AF478574

FREEDOM AT STAKE

Freedom at Stake

A BACKGROUND BOOK

Peter Archer

and

Lord Reay

DUFOUR EDITIONS

CHESTER SPRINGS

PENNSYLVANIA

Library of Congress Catalog Card number: 67–15647
Manufactured in Great Britain
First published in the U.S.A. 1967

CONTENTS

PREFACE

THIS BOOK sets out unashamedly to grind an axe. Its thesis is that in any political system, from the most systematic tyranny to the most enlightened democracy, the individual may sometimes feel himself caught up in an impersonal administrative machine. And unless he is assured both of formal safeguards and of the sympathy of vigilant neighbours the consequences for him may be tragic.

The success of such a book may be measured by the time it takes to become out of date. It is pleasing to record that in two important respects it has already fallen behind events. In December 1965, the United Kingdom government accepted the optional clauses in the European Convention on Human Rights for an experimental period of three years, so that United Kingdom citizens now have the right of individual petition to the European Commission, and their complaint may be argued before the European Court. Secondly, plans have been announced for the appointment in the near future of a Parliamentary Commissioner to investigate complaints of administrative injustice for which the law provides no remedy.

The authors wish to express their appreciation of the assistance they have received from the staff of Amnesty International, who readily made their time available and who were able to provide from their files detailed documentation relating to individual cases. But it is proper to add that in the views expressed the authors represent no one but themselves.

One of the authors, Peter Archer, would like to place on record his obligation to the other, Lord Reay, who was asked to assist when the book had fallen so far behind schedule that there was a danger of indefinite delay. In a very short period he produced the sections in Chapters 3 and 4 relating to Ghana and Portugal, thereby making possible the completion and publication of a book whose relevance to events is essential.

The selection of examples and case histories will inevitably tempt criticism, and all that can be urged in defence is that it represents an honest attempt to study different approaches to the protection of human rights in the writings of the theorists and in the practice of public officials. Inevitably, too, there will be those who regard the portrayal as unfair. If these studies lead to debate, so much the better. For debate is the lifeline of freedom. When debate is hindered or inhibited the lifeline is severed.

London,
August, 1966

PETER ARCHER
REAY

I

The Price of Liberty

WORTHWHILE activities are made possible only by people living together in communities. But living in communities imposes its own restrictions. If a community is to function, if law and order are to be maintained, trade and employment regulated, public hygiene provided for, and help afforded to the old and sick, there must be officials who are charged with these duties. And they must perforce be invested with the power to issue instructions and prohibitions, the power to tax, and the power to arrest.

The purpose of government is to get things done, and if they are to be done efficiently and energetically, officials must be given rights of coercion which can be used as the need arises. Democracy imposes only two requirements. First, it requires that the officials shall carry out a policy decided by the elected representatives of those who are administered. Of course, it may be argued that any given system of recording votes is unsatisfactory, that the choice is at best restricted, that the public is at the mercy of psychological pressure which is not political argument. Suffice it here to suggest that one human right is the right to be consulted.

But even a majority may impose a tyranny. And the second requirement is that the administrators should conform with certain rules, determined by the elected representatives. The rules must be binding upon all officials, and those who complain that they have not been observed must have recourse to the courts, or to some impartial and authoritative tribunal. This will inevitably mean a curtailment of the officials' discretion. It will mean technicality and red tape. And it will encourage the excuse: 'I would like to help you, but there is nothing I can do.' The disadvantage of technicalities is that they restrict the power to distinguish between situations. But that is their function. For the most honest official may sometimes exercise a discretion unfairly or for irrelevant reasons.

All this is, of course, to say nothing of the rules themselves. Carefully drafted rules, adopted by an elected parliament and administered by conscientious officials, may yet prove effective instruments of tyranny if they are in fact tyrannical rules. In particular, they will be tyrannical if they discriminate against a group of people on grounds which are irrelevant to their individual conduct. There must be some discrimination concerning the mentally incapable, the very young, and the anti-social. But to discriminate according to racial characteristics, appearances or culture, is frequently the beginning of the process which leads to the police state. Freedom is indivisible, and to begin by withholding it from some may ensure that in time it will be denied to all.

From the moment when the first regulation treats a human being as something less, the whole framework of democracy is in danger. For one oppressive law will in time require to be supplemented by another. And each new provision will add a further term to the vocabulary of oppression. Worse, it will further inoculate the public conscience.

Already there may be those who object. And if the government has an efficient public relations service it will convince the majority that the objectors are the enemies, not merely of the party in power, but of the people. It will label them 'communists', 'reactionaries', 'socialists', 'liberals', or whatever may be the local term of abuse. But if this fails to silence them, further measures may be required. While the public is still prepared to see them repressed, their publications must be censored, and their meetings banned. If they continue to meet, in defiance of what is now the law, the police will be instructed to interfere. And if, in an excess of zeal, violence is introduced, it may be thought of as no more than they deserve.

The government, the police, and the public will therefore be progressively persuading themselves that these people are dangerous, and that good government, law and order demand emergency measures. If a person suspected of subversive activities cannot be shown to have committed a criminal offence, he may be imprisoned without. And if pressure is used to extract information about his colleagues, it will be justified by its fruits. At this stage the measures adopted will be temporary ones, to meet what is regarded as an emergency. A statute may have been passed, conferring on the government power to make regulations for meeting the emergency, if indeed such an Act was not already lying, unrepealed but half forgotten, in the statute book.

Sometimes emergencies do arise, and energetic measures need to be taken. But it requires the sternest self-discipline on the part of a government to recognise that the emergency has passed, and that they are no longer justified. If the emergency lasts too long, the regulations become a normal part of public administration. The government which envisaged the legislation, the public which condoned it, and the officials who have experienced it as part of their work, are already too deeply committed. When the officials exceed what was originally intended, the government is all too ready to whitewash the events, and the public to pretend that what took place was inevitable. The misfortunes of others are rarely so striking that they cannot be dispelled from our thoughts with a determined effort.

For the public, and even the politicians, the victims of discriminatory legislation are defined by their inclusive label—'negroes', 'jews', 'communists', 'fascists'—and the individuals to whom the description applies are either unknown, or assume at best a shadowy existence. For the officials who must administer the legislation there may sometimes be less excuse, for they often confront them as individuals. And generalisations are more difficult to sustain when one meets the individuals to whom they apply. But the officials have little time for political theory. They are busy men, charged with the duty of making the scheme work. The individuals who incur their attention are merely the details.

Even in countries which do not practise discrimination, and where tyranny is resented, there are opportunities enough for misunderstanding. To a member of the public, regulations and those who apply them are there to serve him. Administrators exist to facilitate his purposes. Administration is not life. Eating and working, football and gardens, picnics and music, worship and sex, beer and skittles—these things are life. Paying taxes, serving on juries, completing census forms—these are interruptions to the business of living. They must be done, and without them there can be no living. But the wrappings must not be confused with their contents.

For the official, on the contrary, administering is his daily work. What the ordinary man regards as unnecessary irritations are for him the tools of his trade. The registrar's forms, the lawyer's technicalities, the policeman's notebook, are to them what the micrometer is to the engineer. The official has a duty to perform, and upon its performance rests the public welfare, perhaps the public safety. Under pressure, when the volume of work demands that each case shall be dealt with quickly, when resistance is merely a nuisance, and resisters often offensive and unreasonable, he is tempted to treat an objecting citizen as the carpenter treats a recalcitrant piece of wood. Many a horrifying act of tyranny has been committed because it seemed a good idea at the time.

Human rights are often endangered not by wicked men, but by prejudiced men or sometimes by harassed men. This is the justification for laying down rules limiting their discretion. And it may justify, too, limitations upon the government itself. There have been attempts to formulate precisely, as rules of government, those aspirations which are normally, and vaguely, referred to as civil rights, natural law, or the rights of man.

But no rules will prevent a determined government which seeks systematically the destruction of all human rights. Nor can they always prevent the accidental lapse. Ultimately, human rights can have no safeguard but human compassion. And their lifeblood is the humanity of those who administer, and of the public which chooses its administrators. Human problems have much in common. Those with no interest in how a man lives his life will shed no tears when he suffers tyranny. The politician who gleans no pleasure from watching the sun set over his garden, or from telling a story to a child, will never become a master of his craft, for he has no understanding of its raw materials. But no less heartless is the gardener or storyteller who knows no concern on learning that another man is denied such pleasures. For he should understand what is denied.

Certainly, regulations protecting individuals, or even a general reluctance to treat them harshly, may sometimes prove an obstacle to policy. Instead of concentrating their energies on the rapid achievement of the final aims, officials are required to stop and consider the interests of particular men and women. The choice is sometimes expressed as one between vigorous government and slower progress. But any vigorous government which enjoys the participation of the public in its aims will be unlikely to ignore such considerations. A lively political community, vigorous and imaginative, is one which watches carefully for infringements against individuals.

2

The Rule of Law

AN ELECTED government is responsible to its electors. If they find its activities shocking, they have their remedy. And, through the government, they control their civil servants, their police and their prison warders. Some things, of course, may be kept secret, and there is no method of controlling what remains hidden, but it is usually possible to ensure that normal administration takes place in the open. Certainly a systematic tyranny cannot for long remain unsuspected unless the public are deliberately deaf.

But may there be a further appeal? The twentieth century has witnessed a succession of nations achieving power to conduct their own affairs. And the process has been welcomed, justifiably, as the expression of freedom. Yet unfettered national sovereignty entails two possibilities which are less attractive to lovers of freedom. It may mean the freedom of one nation to endanger that of others, either by military or economic action; and the freedom of a national government to oppress its own subjects. For nations, as for individuals, it seems that controls are sometimes required. And the democrat hopes not for anarchy, but for rules and authorities set up by the common agreement of those concerned.

Controls upon the freedom of nations to injure others have taken such forms as the United Nations Organisation, the International Court of Justice, and the General Agreement on Tariffs and Trade. And as yet they are not always effective. But limits upon the freedom of a government to destroy freedom within its own borders are at an even earlier stage. International Law is said to govern relationships between states, and between one state and the subjects of another. But the rights and duties of a government towards its own subjects are a matter for its civil law, which may be changed or preserved according to the vagaries of its own internal politics.

And international lawyers have felt the reluctance of us all to interfere where we may not be welcome.

Events in Nazi-occupied Europe raised these questions in a compelling form. At Nuremberg the principle was proclaimed that certain kinds of tyranny are the concern of the whole world. And after the War, those faced with the task of implementing the 'Four Freedoms' recognised that the defeat of one tyrant was not necessarily the end of the problem. But they were pioneers in a new field. The most promising path was to secure such agreement as was possible, to formulate the agreed standards as rules, and to invoke public opinion against governments which transgressed them. The difficulty was that a wide measure of agreement could be secured only by formulating the rules as vaguely as possible. And there is rarely a clear breach of a rule which is itself unclear.

The United Nations Charter, setting out the post-war aims of the Allied nations, afforded a prominent place to this aspiration. Article 1 sets out as one of the purposes of the United Nations:

> 'To achieve international co-operation . . . in promoting and encouraging respect for human rights and for fundamental freedoms for all, without distinction as to race, sex, language, or religion . . .'

A Commission on Human Rights was set up, under Mrs Eleanor Roosevelt, with instructions to draft a bill of human rights, setting out rules on which all members of the United Nations could agree. By 1948 the introductory part of the bill was prepared, and on 10 December 1948, the General Assembly adopted it (by 48 votes to nil, with eight abstentions), as the Universal Declaration of Human Rights. 10 December has since been commemorated each year as Human Rights Day. Admittedly the commemorations have not attracted wide attention, but this may be due less to a lack of interest in human rights than to the overloading of the calendar with anniversaries.

The Universal Declaration was intended to set out the minimum duties which a government could be said to owe to each of its citizens. It asserted such positive economic rights as the free choice of employment, without discrimination, the right to an adequate standard of living and social services, and to participation in the cultural life of the community. The hopes which it embodied were expressed by the President of the General Assembly, Dr H. V. Evatt of Australia, himself an eminent lawyer:

> 'It is the first occasion on which the organized community of nations has made a declaration of human rights and fundamental freedoms, and it has the authority of the body of opinion of the United Nations as a whole, and millions of men, women and children all over the world, many miles from Paris and New York, will turn for help, guidance and inspiration to this document.'

As a legal document it suffered from three defects. It was not drafted in the form of a treaty, to be ratified by member states, and it therefore appears not to be binding in International Law. It is a Declaration, setting out standards which members recognise as morally incumbent. Secondly, although carefully drafted, the Declaration does not purport to set out rules with the precision necessary if any government is to be convicted of a clear breach. Thirdly, it contains no machinery for enforcing its provisions. There is no authority to whom the victim of a breach might complain; no tribunal to decide whether his complaint is justified; and no action prescribed by way of redress.

Not that the Commission was to blame. The Declaration had been intended merely as the preamble to a bill of human rights. The remainder of the bill was to consist of two parts; a covenant on human rights, which should formulate the duties of governments more precisely, and which should be legally binding upon those who accepted it; and 'measures of implementation', supplying the bill with teeth by setting up machinery of enforcement.

The Commission proceeded with the remainder of the bill. On the instructions of the General Assembly, two separate covenants were drafted, one setting out 'civil and political rights', corresponding with Articles 3 to 21 of the Declaration, and one 'economic, social and cultural rights', corresponding with Articles 22 to 27. Each covenant contained its own measures of implementation.

The Commission recommended that a human rights committee should be set up to receive complaints relating to civil and political rights. The committee would investigate the dispute with a view to suggesting an amicable solution, and failing settlement, there should be a right to bring the matter before the International Court of Justice. In the case of economic, social and cultural rights, states would merely bind themselves to take steps towards their full realisation to the maximum of their resources, and implementation would take the form of periodic reports to the Economic and Social Council of the United Nations. The preliminary drafts were ready by 1954, but the final texts have not yet been agreed by the General Assembly, and it now seems that any prospect of general agreement is receding.

The Human Rights Programme has not remained at a standstill. In 1956 member states were asked to submit reports every three years to the Economic and Social Council, specifying measures taken and progress achieved in safeguarding human rights within their own territories. The reports are examined by the Commission, which submits recommendations to the Council, but does not pass judgment on specific governments. The Council and the Commission have also undertaken studies of specific topics relating to human rights. And there have been seminars for the exchange of ideas, and scholarships to promote study of the subject. In addition, there are advisory services, to offer expert assistance at the request of governments, where guidance has not already been provided. Each year information relating to human rights is brought up to date in the Year Book of Human Rights.

There have been conventions on particular aspects of the subject, based upon the Declaration, and recognised as binding by the states who have ratified them. There are conventions relating to the prevention of genocide, to the protection of refugees and stateless persons, to the abolition of forced labour, and to slavery. And the Declaration has been cited in a number of resolutions by the General Assembly, particularly resolutions relating to South Africa. The effect has been to focus public opinion on these matters. Already suggestions have been made for the appointment some day of a United Nations attorney-general—an ombudsman of human rights.

International agreements, even when they are binding in International Law, do not alter the domestic (or internal) law of any country unless the state itself provides for it, but a number of legal systems have been influenced by the Declaration. Provisions from the Declaration have been incorporated into a number of constitutions, notably those of Indonesia, Libya and Nigeria. In many countries there has been legislation on specific topics in which the Declaration has been expressly cited. And the effect on legal opinion has appeared in a number of individual decisions in which courts have cited the Declaration as part of their reasons.

But the fact remains that progress since 1948 has disappointed those who then worked with such enthusiasm. Until the Conventions on Human Rights are adopted by the General Assembly, the most promising development is the acceptance of more concrete measures by particular groups of countries. And the possibilities have been indicated in Western Europe. Whatever the political differences among Western European nations, most of them hold views on police states which are sufficiently uniform to achieve a measure of detailed agreement.

And on 4 November 1950, the Consultative Assembly for the Council of Europe, meeting in Rome, adopted a Convention for the Protection of Human Rights and Fundamental Freedoms. The Preamble recited that the participants agree: 'being resolved, as the governments of European countries which are like-minded and have a common heritage of political traditions, ideals, freedom and the rule of law, to take the first steps for the collective enforcement of certain of the rights stated in the Universal Declaration.'

The Convention sets out its rules in much greater detail

than the Universal Declaration, though the number of topics with which it deals is more limited, since questions on which agreement was impossible were eliminated. The Convention is binding in International Law upon those members of the Council of Europe who have ratified it. Of the fifteen members of the Council, only France has so far failed to ratify it.

A great achievement of the Convention was that agreement was reached upon machinery for enforcement. It provided for the establishment of a European Commission of Human Rights, and in May 1954 the Commission was set up. Its fifteen members are appointed by the Committee of Ministers of the Council of Europe, and no country is to have more than one of its nationals as a member. The Commission has established itself, with a secretariat, in Strasbourg.

It receives complaints in the form of petitions addressed to the Secretary-General of the Council of Europe. Under Article 24 of the Convention, a petition may be presented by any party to the Convention (that is, by any state which has signed and ratified it). Article 25 empowers it also to receive petitions from 'any person, non-governmental organisation or group of individuals claiming to be the victim of a violation', but only if the government against whom the petition is presented has declared its acceptance of this provision. Article 25 was to operate only after at least six states accepted the provision, and in fact it came into operation in July 1955. The states which have accepted the provision are: Belgium, Denmark, Iceland, Norway, Sweden and Western Germany.

The Convention provides that the Commission 'shall' receive petitions under Article 24, while Article 25 provides merely that the Commission 'may' receive petitions to which it applies. In the former case, the petition is investigated by a sub-commission, consisting of members of the Commission. The sub-commission then reports to the Commission, which discusses the matter with the parties concerned, in the hope of reaching a mutually satisfactory solution. (The assumption is that parties to the Rome Convention are not deliberately and systematically pursuing acts of tyranny, but may be guilty of occasional lapses.) The Commission then reports to the Council of Ministers, outlining the settlement, if one has been reached, or otherwise making its recommendations. The final decision rests with the Council of Ministers, and parties to the Convention are bound by their direction.

Fears have repeatedly been expressed that the right of individual recourse under Article 25 would lead to a flood of petitions from cranks and 'barrack-room lawyers', demanding time and expense, and embarrassing the governments concerned. Indeed, copious correspondence has been received from men who imagined themselves victimised. This risk is incidental to any provision safeguarding individual liberty, and the problem was to preserve the right intact without devoting undue time to those petitions which were manifestly without merit, or clearly outside the competence of the Commission. Accordingly, the Commission has laid down a procedure by which petitions under Article 25 are examined by a group of three members of the Commission. The group then reports to the full Commission, which decides whether the application is admissible. Reference is not made to the government against which the complaint is presented unless the application appears, on the surface, to be admissible. By far the majority of petitions so far received under Article 25 have been rejected at once.

The Commission has formulated a number of rules with which a complaint must comply if it is to be considered. In particular, the complaint must purport to refer to a specific violation of the Convention, arising after the Convention came into force in 1953, and the applicant must have exhausted all his remedies within the legal system of the country against which the complaint is made.

But the last word is with the Council of Ministers, and the Council consists of politicians. Politicians are not the most suitable people to decide when rules have been broken, and what to do about it. They can hardly avoid fixing half an eye on the political consequences of their decision. And in any event they have other matters to occupy their time. An impartial tribunal consisting of lawyers may be slow and irritating, but it is at least more likely to decide the question in dispute, and decide it on the evidence.

The Convention therefore made further provision for a European Court of Human Rights. It was to consist of fifteen judges, elected by the Consultative Assembly of the Council from names submitted by the member states. The Court was to hear cases referred to it by the Commission or by any member state (though not directly by private individuals) but only against a state which has accepted the Court's jurisdiction, either in the particular matter, or compulsorily in all cases. It was provided that the Court was not to be set up until at least eight member states had accepted the compulsory jurisdiction. That condition was fulfilled in September 1958, and in January 1959 the judges were elected. The first international tribunal of human rights was established.

The countries which have so far accepted the compulsory jurisdiction are: Austria, Belgium, Denmark, Iceland, Luxembourg, the Netherlands, and Western Germany.

It is too early to assess the effectiveness of the Court, and the kind of jurisprudence which it is likely to construct. Some indication appears from the fate of Gerard Richard Lawless, a Southern Irishman who was detained without charge or trial by the Eire Government for nine months, as a suspected member of the IRA. He complained to the Commission, which held that the application was prima facie admissible. In due course, the Commission referred the case to the Court, which heard argument from Professor Waldock, Chairman of the Commission, from the Irish Attorney-General and, although Lawless himself was not technically a party to the proceedings (which were brought by the Commission), from his legal adviser. The Irish government urged that the detention was justified by the existence of public danger, and finally the Court accepted the explanation. It was held that the detention was justified and that there had been no breach of the Convention.

This is the only case to date in which the Court has given judgment. But the Commission has shown that it is capable of effective action, and a government which has accepted the jurisdiction of the Court will be limited to measures which it can justify.

The European experiment has already proved sufficiently effective to encourage suggestions for further Conventions. There has been a proposal for an All-American Court of Human Rights. And it is by no means visionary to conceive of a British Commonwealth Court. The withdrawal of South Africa from the Commonwealth may establish the principle that membership entails the acceptance of certain standards. If so, agreement should be possible as to what those standards are. Until such a proposal is made by a Commonwealth government, speculation on its probable fate is pointless.

Meanwhile, a number of privately sponsored societies are drawing attention to breaches of the Universal Declaration. Among those which have for many years directed public opinion to particular aspects of the subject are the International Commission of Jurists, the Anti-Slavery League, the International League for the Rights of Man, the Congress for Cultural Freedom, the Commonwealth Press Association, the International Press Association and Amnesty International.

It may be hoped that in time respect for individual freedom will be protected by formal safeguards, recognised in International Law, enforced in international tribunals, and accepted as binding by the legislative and judicial organs of national governments. But as yet the key to human rights has not been delivered to lawyers, for they can only apply existing rules. And those who would challenge the right of a government to treat as its own a human body or a human soul are committed to a political argument.

On 28 August 1961 the Ghana Supreme Court ruled that the Preventive Detention Act was none the less valid because it may conflict with the solemn declaration of fundamental human rights made by President Nkrumah on assuming office. 'The people's remedy for any departure from the principles of the declaration', said the Court, 'is through the ballot box and not through the Courts.' It might have added that, where the remedy is left unused, it may be only a matter of time before the ballot box itself is no longer available.

3
Some Views on Human Rights

The United Kingdom

SINCE LONG before they first purported to record them, Englishmen have asserted their 'ancient liberties'. They, and their fellow Britons, have vociferously denied the suggestion that they ever shall be slaves, and have accorded their country the title 'Mother of the Free'.

Yet there is no formal limitation upon the powers of the Parliamentary majority. A statute revoking the right to Habeas Corpus, abolishing trial by jury, or reintroducing the Star Chamber, would have the full force of law, and would require no greater formality than an Act abolishing dog licences. Nor does the ballot box provide a complete remedy, since any Parliament would be entitled, by passing a simple Act, to delay the next Election indefinitely.

Asked, then, how this tradition of freedom arises, it is common to ascribe it to three great political documents: Magna Carta, the Petition of Right, and the Bill of Rights. None of them purported to introduce new rights. Each claimed merely to re-state what had long been recognised. And none of them is in any way binding in law upon the parliamentary majority. Magna Carta is the earliest, and certainly that document helped to establish that the English do not merely presume, but delight, to turn any temporary difficulty of their government into an occasion for the redress of grievances. In 1215 the economic troubles of King John led him forcibly to seize his subjects' money, and thus to make inroads upon customs which until then had been scarcely noticed. Interrupted, they transpired to be dear to those who had enjoyed them. And a process of political manœuvre and counter-intrigue compelled the King to issue a statement drafted by his opponents.

Magna Carta has become the symbol of an important process. People who have enjoyed a practice for many years do not look upon it as a privilege, or even as the exercise of a right. But if it is interrupted, the best and the most cussed among them voice objections. From their bickerings a right is born. And when that right is expressed in the language of a great draftsman, it becomes a principle. The safeguard against its infringement, whether by a dictator or a Parliamentary majority, is that it becomes so much part of public thinking that politicians (who are, after all, members of the public) would not seek to infringe it, and if they did, they would meet the resistance of officials, police and public alike.

The conception of individual rights was not handed down to the British people on tablets of stone. It was rough-hewn into everyday life with the grumbles of men and women by working lawyers and politicians. So each generation, in the course of managing its own business, contributed to the future.

Conscious political theory as a means of questioning the power of the government is scarcely earlier in the British Isles than the seventeenth century, when successively in Scotland and England the Stuarts, like a succession of tyrants since, rendered a great service to the cause of human rights in challenging people to formulate them. But if the battle was fought against the Stuarts, the forces had been mobilised centuries earlier. Parliament was already an ancient institution, and it was its embodiment of a familiar idea, rather than the inherent justice of representative government, which assured to it the loyalty of its members and a respect in the country.

Possibly the greatest single contribution to the cause of liberty in England was the Statute of Northampton, 1328. Already the king's function of deciding disputes was assigned to men who made it their life's work, and brought to their task a technical, and often pedantic, professionalism. In the course of doing their job, they constructed their own instrument, the Common Law. In 1328 the King and his Council ordained that for the future no royal command should disturb the course of the Common Law. It was many generations later before judges felt safe in applying the statute literally, but a clear distinction had been created between those who govern and those who pass judgment. And during the great debates between the Stuarts and their Parliaments, there were in existence a body of men capable of formulating the case for asserting that governmental officials, even kings and their ministers, are subject to the rules. They did so by appealing to the Common Law of England, which even then carried an authority in men's minds as great as the authority of a crown and sceptre.

The royalists were defeated in debate by men like Coke, who over the years had done their day's work in listening to the complaints of ordinary people, and their homework in dusty legal archives, and like Prynne, who having weakened his eyesight in studying the Yearbooks by candlelight, was prepared to lose his ears for proclaiming what he had learned. The claims of the absolutists were defeated, case by case, in the courts; the independence of the courts was defended (sometimes at the cost of martyrdom) by politicians who were only beginning to understand the significance of the struggle; and their stand was supported by thousands who dimly associated the Common Law with an established way of life in which they had not been subjected to acts of tyranny against their homes and their pockets.

'Hundreds of Englishmen who hated toleration and cared little for freedom of speech entertained a keen jealousy of arbitrary power, and a fixed determination to be ruled in accordance with the law of the land.' So, in 1883, wrote Dicey of his seventeenth-century forebears. It was not always seen as a victory of modern enlightenment over outmoded privilege. Francis Bacon, observing the process as a contemporary, saw it as the frustration of vigorous government by the technical conservatism of the common lawyers. Yet this was the period when principles were formulated, and thus the victory over absolutism assured after the particular conditions which had given rise to the arguments had passed away. When they were no longer needed to denounce despotic kings, they could be called into action against Parliamentary leaders, and judges, and their agents. Thus in the distant future was vigorous government made possible without an inevitable tyranny.

So, if principles in Britain emerged from everyday life, they have affected the everyday life of the future. The British display a contempt for general declarations, which lack specific means for their enforcement. Dicey described the Habeas Corpus Acts as 'for practical purposes worth a hundred constitutional articles guaranteeing individual liberty'. Yet this sweeping pronouncement is only half the truth. Had there never been a statement of principle about individual liberty, half the debates, in the courts and in Parliament, relating to the application of the Habeas Corpus Acts, would not have been possible. Slavery in England was finally declared abolished upon applications for habeas corpus, but the applications were granted by judges who hated the idea of slavery.

Hence, too, the general principle that speech in Britain is free, and the concentration of subsequent debate upon particular exceptions. Under the Stuarts, printing presses required to be licensed. To print and publish without the consent of the licensers was an offence punished by the Star Chamber. In 1641 the Parliamentary party struck a successful blow for liberty by securing the abolition of the Star Chamber, but their immediate reaction was merely to transfer control of the press to their own hands. In 1643 the House of Commons authorised its Committee of Examination to establish its own licensing system. In protest against this, Milton wrote *Areopagitica*, which stands as a reasoned argument that political debate is not merely something to be tolerated, but a practice to be welcomed, as a means of ventilating proposals for improving life, and of arriving at truth.

The censorship continued, and when power changed hands again with the Restoration, and again with the Revolution of 1688, the only effect upon the licensing system was that persecuted and persecutors exchanged positions. In 1695, the House of Commons declined to renew the Licensing Act, despite the disapproval of the Lords, but their reasons were concerned less with the principles enunciated by Milton than with the muddle and delay in the operation of the system.

Yet posterity awarded the debate to Milton. Since 1695, there has been no restriction upon the publication of anything which a man may write, provided that he can afford to print and distribute it, or can persuade someone who possesses the necessary resources to do so. True, he is answerable after the publication for any breach of the law, and there remain fields, such as the law relating to obscenity, in which it is debatable whether the law goes further than is required, and the licensing of stage plays, in which there is a wide executive discretion outside the rules of law. But in Britain the burden of establishing a case is always felt to lie upon those who, in a particular instance, seek to limit free speech.

An advantage of relying upon principles enshrined in public consciousness, rather than upon constitutional norms, is that they adapt themselves more readily to changing conditions. One such change has been particularly noticeable in Britain during the late nineteenth and twentieth centuries. Dicey referred to it as the growth of collectivism, and even that sturdy Liberal admitted that it was possible to look upon men too exclusively as separate persons. There are some freedoms which can be preserved only by planning the resources of the community as a whole, although this must entail some restriction upon the freedom of men to make their individual decisions. The change has led inevitably to certain extensions of governmental control, both at the expense of Parliament (hence the debate as to the proper limits of delegated legislation) and of the Courts (giving rise to a succession of cautions about the dangers of administrative tribunals). The truth is dawning that the freedom of human beings to live as they wish may be as much endangered by the tyranny of employers or trade unions, the rapacity of slum landlords, incursions upon privacy by the Press, the activities of high-pressure salesmen, or the selfishness of drivers, as it is by government. And the human mind is as sensitive to social pressure as it is to official censorship.

But if the British approach is more flexible, it is for that very reason less effective in matters which do not impinge upon the public sufficiently to focus opinion. With the exception of a few M.P.s, the British public displayed little interest in the events which led to Hola, or to 'Operation Sunrise' in Nyasaland in early 1959, later described in the Report of the Devlin Commission. And when public opinion stirs, it is sometimes made aware of the facts too late.

The British remain unimpressed by formal declarations. While British delegates participated enthusiastically in the work of the Commission, the Universal Declaration occasioned little notice in British newspapers. Even *The Times**, having briefly noticed the acceptance of the Declaration, devoted what little space remained to reporting 'a long and bitter attack . . . by the Soviet group against the Declaration . . .' (a report which, incidentally, over-simplified the Russian attitude).

And the United Kingdom has shown a marked reluctance to accept what successive governments have regarded as limitations upon national sovereignty entailed in the European Convention. It has refused to declare acceptance of the right of individual recourse under Article 25 of the Convention, and when Dr Hastings Banda of Nyasaland wished to complain against his detention, he was compelled to ask the Icelandic government to present a petition as a party to the Convention, under Article 24. The Icelandic government refused. Nor has the United Kingdom accepted the jurisdiction of the European Court of Human Rights. The attitude of the post-war Labour Government was stated baldly in the House of Commons† by the Foreign Secretary, Mr Ernest Bevin.

'We have not undertaken at this stage to sign the optional clause. We think that in this country, with our obligations not only at home but overseas, our procedure for appeals stands very high, and we are not prepared without further thought, to hand over those appeal rights to another body.'

Seven years later‡ Mr Selwyn Lloyd declared the attitude of a Conservative government in very similar terms.

> 'The position which Her Majesty's Government have continuously taken up is that they do not recognise the right of individual petition, because they take the view that states are

* 11 December 1948.
† 13 November 1950.
‡ 29 July 1957.

the proper subject of international law and if individuals are given rights under international treaties effect should be given to those rights through the law of the states concerned. The reason why we do not accept the idea of the compulsory jurisdiction of a European Court is that it would mean that British codes of common and statute law would be subject to review by an international Court. For many years, it has been the position of successive British Governments that we should not accept that status.'

The British profess contempt for declarations without means of enforcement. But, asked to subscribe to a means of enforcement, the view of successive British governments continues to be that, for individual citizens of the United Kingdom and Colonies, there should be no recourse against successive British governments.

The United States

The United States was born of a revolt in the name of freedom against what its people considered to be a tyrannical government. It is not surprising, therefore, that its people were concerned chiefly to ensure that their own administrators should never be capable of a similar tyranny.

Unlike Britain, which evolved a system of government over a long period without noticing what it was doing, the United States was projected at birth into a modern world which demanded ready-made institutions. Its founders had, therefore, to decide consciously what those institutions should be and, having opted for a particular design, to incorporate it into a form of words. So, in 1787, there assembled in Philadelphia the delegates from the various states, to draft the new constitution.

For sixteen weeks they debated what they considered to be the principal issues; the relative powers of the states and the Federation; and the merits and dangers of 'democracy' (by which they meant extending the franchise to those without property and education). Then, the draft completed, they returned to their state conventions, and the debates began afresh as the states were invited to ratify the new document. Critics of the draft Constitution pointed out, correctly, that it imposed no limit upon the powers of either state or federal government over individuals.

'I do not like . . . the omission of a bill of rights, providing clearly, and without the aid of sophism, for freedom of religion, freedom of the press . . . the eternal and unremitting force for the habeas corpus laws, and trials by jury in all matters of fact triable by the laws of the land . . . I have a right to nothing, which another has a right to take away; and Congress will have a right to take away trials by jury in all civil cases.* Let me add, that a bill of rights is what the people are entitled to against every government on earth, general or particular; and what no just government should refuse, or rest on inference.' So wrote Thomas Jefferson, later to be President, to James Madison.

Finally, the supporters of the Constitution secured its ratification in all the states, but in many cases by very narrow majorities, and only upon their promise to introduce at once by way of amendment to the Constitution a Bill of Rights. And there were duly introduced into the first Congress, and passed, the first ten amendments to the Constitution, still referred to as the Bill of Rights.

In terms they afford a guarantee of almost all the rights which appear in the great constitutional documents of the United Kingdom. But there remained the vital question: what was to happen if the government sought to disregard them. It was not answered until 1803, when the case of Marbury *v.* Madison came before the Supreme Court presided over by Chief Justice Marshall, like Coke a man whose strength of character has exercised greater influence on history than the learning and logic of many more brilliant men. Confronted by a provision in a federal statute which exceeded the powers conferred on the federal government by the Constitution, he declared the provision void.

* To a great extent, the governments of the United States and the United Kingdom have subsequently done so, without any obvious loss of liberty.

'To what purpose are powers limited, and to what purpose is that limitation committed to writing,' he demanded, 'if these limits may, at any time, be passed by those intended to be restrained? . . . The Constitution is either a superior paramount law, unchangeable by ordinary means, or it is on a level with ordinary legislative Acts, and, like other Acts, is alterable when the legislature shall please to alter it. If the former part of the alternative be true, then a legislative Act contrary to the Constitution is not law; if the latter part be true, then written constitutions are absurd attempts, on the part of the people, to limit a power in its own nature illimitable.'

Since that judgment, no Act of Congress, and no executive action of the President, has been enforceable if, in the view of the Supreme Court, it conflicts with the Constitution. The Bill of Rights undoubtedly stands between the government and the citizen. But it is drafted in the sweeping terms of a general declaration rather than the precise clauses of a statute, and the constructions laid upon it have sometimes reflected nothing more venerable than the political views of the judges who heard the case. In the 1930s, a conservative Supreme Court argued from certain Constitutional provisions to declare invalid a series of measures imposing governmental control on business interests. Yet if it has sometimes imposed a fetter upon vigorous economic policies, the Bill has undoubtedly helped to perpetuate those ideas of fairness which inspired such men as Jefferson.

The United States has a distinguished record in securing the international recognition of human rights. The drafting of the Universal Declaration is largely the work of minds trained in the construction of the United States Constitution, and the earliest measures of agreement were largely the result of Mrs Roosevelt's personality. Not that her enthusiasm has been universal among Americans. In 1953 the Republican administration announced that it would not sign any United Nations treaty implementing the Declaration.

A field where Americans are sharply divided in their views, both on the Constitution and on human rights, is that which concerns the position of the coloured population. Until 1863, any legal protection afforded to the vast majority of them was designed for the benefit of their owners, who looked to the law to protect their property. Even the minority who were not slaves were virtually devoid of legal status. In the Dred Scott case, of 1857, the Supreme Court ruled that the draftsmen of the Constitution did not intend the words 'people' and 'citizen' to apply to coloured people.

In 1863, slavery was abolished in the United States, and after the Civil War, while the South was occupied by Federal forces, negroes were accorded civil rights. In 1868 was passed the Fourteenth Amendment to the Constitution, which declared, among other similar provisions, that 'no state shall ... deny to any person within its jurisdiction the equal protection of the law'. And in 1870 the Fifteenth Amendment prescribed that the right to vote 'shall not be denied or abridged ... on account of race (or) colour...'.

In 1877 the occupation terminated, and the southern states exacted their revenge upon the coloured population. Laws were passed imposing complete segregation in public places.*

The Fifteenth Amendment was evaded by imposing upon the franchise such property and educational qualifications that most coloured people could not hope to satisfy them. And even those who did were subjected to social pressure, and often violence, to discourage them from registering. As late as 1963, of over 422,000 coloured people who were eligible to vote in Mississippi, only 28,500 were registered. Segregation was enforced rigidly in the schools. Here again, facilities, though separate, were asserted to be equal. It merely arose in practice that there were not usually sufficient funds to provide two decent school buildings in an area, and naturally it was the coloured children who had to be content with the dilapidated one. So it was with equipment, and staff.

From time to time indignant negroes and sympathetic whites found methods of protesting, and in 1909 there was

* In 1896 the Supreme Court ruled that there was no breach of the Fourteenth Amendment in providing 'separate but equal' facilities in transport services.

founded the National Association for the Advancement of Coloured People. It was they who assisted the parents of children attending Scott's School, Summerton in South Carolina, to challenge in the courts, and finally up to the Supreme Court, the right of the local school board to confine coloured children to a school where there were 105 children in one class. In 1954 the Supreme Court decided that 'separate educational facilities are inherently unequal'. In the next ten years, resources were made available to challenge one disability after another, and the Supreme Court condemned as unconstitutional discrimination in inter-state travel facilities, in restaurants serving inter-state customers, and in hospitals; the exclusion of coloured people from juries; the practice in legal proceedings of addressing coloured people by their first names; and the failure to assign counsel to people accused of serious crimes.

The Supreme Court has been accused of having been infiltrated by Communists, and there has been an attempt to impeach the Chief Justice. The 1954 decision on education led to a series of devices designed to evade the ruling. Georgia and South Carolina decided to cease spending money on public education, thus compelling children to attend private schools which would, of course, be segregated. Then they would spend the equivalent sum in providing 'tuition grants' towards the upkeep of the private schools. The Richmond (Virginia) *News Leader* suggested 'a long course of lawful resistance; it is to take lawful advantage of every moment of the law's delays; it is to seek at the polls and in the halls of legislative bodies every possible lawful means to overcome or circumvent the Court's requirements. Litigate? Let us pledge ourselves to litigate this thing for fifty years. If one remedial law is ruled invalid, then let us enact a third (*sic*).'

The legal profession looked forward to a period of prosperity. But some kinds of resistance displayed less respect for legal forms. Coloured children who attended some of the desegregated schools were subjected to a course of bullying, until they withdrew. Coloured people who registered as electors were beaten up and their homes burned. Those, coloured and white, who have taken part in demonstrations have been mobbed, arrested and manhandled by the police, and imprisoned for obstruction, parading without a permit or a similar offence. More than once, civil rights workers have been murdered, but Southern juries have refused to convict those arrested for them.

Happily, there are many Americans whose views, though opposite, are equally strong. These questions, as Southern politicians have continued to reiterate, have traditionally been considered to be under the control of the states. Between 1877 and 1954, the Federal government studiously avoided interfering, but following the lead of the Supreme Court, the Federal Department of Justice has now made clear its intention to enforce the Constitution. Not that it has been sufficiently vigorous to satisfy civil rights leaders. The Department has been reluctant to overrule state responsibility for law and order by invoking special federal powers, and the difficulty of securing a conviction from a Southern jury for violence against coloured people or civil rights workers has sometimes discouraged it from pursuing prosecutions. But officials of the Department have consistently helped coloured people in securing registration as voters, and have pointed out that this, if achieved, will deliver into their hands the power to insist upon the redress of other grievances.

In 1964, after what had threatened to become an endless filibuster by the conservatives, the government secured the passage through Congress of the Civil Rights Act, making discrimination illegal in public accommodation, education, employment, and voting lists. The discriminators are still prepared for a long battle. But the campaign song of the Civil Rights campaigners, 'We shall overcome', appears already to be coming true. The struggle has helped to vindicate the Supreme Court and, somewhat belatedly, the Federal government, as champions of human rights. And the very fact that the debate is proving to be protracted is largely because the Constitution ensured, in the interests of democracy, that even an elected national government cannot take for granted that it will always have its own way.

'The capitalist law is based upon the abstract "natural rights" of an individual; it places the individual in the centre of the world, surrounds him with a cult and therefore establishes limits to the State. . . . However, the proletarian state sets the limits not to itself but to its citizens. A collective body called the State, rather than the individual citizen, is at the centre of the proletarian law.

'The government has granted rights to citizens not in the name of abstract rights of man . . . but exclusively for its own purpose.'*

Thus, in 1927, an important commentary on the Soviet Civil Code stated the corollary of Soviet theory. For the Marxist, history consists essentially in successive struggles between economic classes. The State, the machinery of government, and the legal system, are all weapons employed by the dominant class to exploit others, and when the exploited class itself seizes power, it must employ them ruthlessly for its own purposes. There then begins the period in which the working class sets about liquidating its former exploiters (as a class—not necessarily by destroying each individual member). But they, for their part, will resist with every weapon available. When they have been finally beaten, there will be no classes, since there will be no groups whose economic interests are opposed to those of the whole people. And there will then be no necessity for these weapons. The State, the legal system, even government itself, will wither away, leaving only (almost as an afterthought) the need for some 'technical regulation'.

This is not the place to examine the validity of the theory. It is the view to which the present Soviet government subscribes. We live now in the period between the Revolution and the final withering away, the period characterised by Lenin as 'the Dictatorship of the Proletariat'. It is the period when the proletariat imposes its own rule, but since it must express its wishes through some more clearly defined

* A. L. Malitsky.

mouthpiece, it is represented by (or rather, equated with) the Communist Party. In 'The State and Revolution', Lenin defined the expression 'the Dictatorship of the Proletariat' as 'unrestricted power, beyond the law, resting on force'.

In 1936, the USSR adopted a new constitution, which on a first reading bears remarkable similarities to, say, the American Bill of Rights. But it was not suggested that this represented a change in Soviet theory. In fact, it was expressly declared to correspond with the existing practice. Introducing the draft, Stalin made no secret that it preserved 'the régime of the dictatorship of the proletariat, just as it preserves unchanged the present leading position of the Communist Party of the USSR'.

Thus the Constitution guaranteed universal suffrage, by secret ballot, for elections to the Supreme Soviet. But the right to nominate candidates was permitted only to specified types of organisation, and the Communist Party was declared to be 'the leading core of all organisations of the working people, both public and state'. (In practice, only one name appears on the ballot paper for each constituency, and nominations rest with the Communist Party.)

Freedom of speech, freedom of the press, and freedom of association, were all guaranteed, but only "in conformity with the interests of the working people and in order to strengthen the socialist system'. There was to be no arrest except by order of a court or of a procurator, and there were provisions guaranteeing the integrity of the home and of private correspondence. But no means of enforcing these rights was provided. The Russian courts have no habeas corpus.

At the very time when the new Constitution was adopted, the NKVD, the secret police organisation which, in 1934, had succeeded the notorious OGPU, was arresting without trial thousands who were believed, rightly or wrongly, to be enemies of the people, including many who had been leaders of the Communist Party in the Revolution, and who were believed by Stalin to be possible rivals. Describing the methods used on Stalin's instructions, Mr Khrushchev read to the Twentieth

Party Congress in 1956 a telegram sent by Stalin to various officials in 1937.

'The Central Committee of the All-Union Communist Party explains that the application of methods of physical pressure in NKVD practice is permissible from 1937 on, in accordance with permission of the Central Committee. . . . It is known that all bourgeois intelligence services use methods of physical influence against the representatives of the socialist proletariat and that they use them in their most scandalous forms. The question arises as to why the Socialist intelligence service should be more humanitarian against the mad agents of the bourgeoisie. . . . The Central Committee . . . considers that physical pressure should still be used obligatorily, as an exception applicable to known and obstinate enemies of the people, as a method both justifiable and appropriate.' He did not explain how it was to be known who were enemies of the people before physical pressure had been used. According to Mr Khrushchev, the telegram was sent without the knowledge or approval of the Central Committee.

Kedrov, one of the revolutionary leaders, was tried and, after prolonged imprisonment and torture, was acquitted, but was nevertheless shot by the NKVD. It is believed that between eight and ten million people died or disappeared in the purges between 1937 and 1939, including many of the ablest administrators. Russia came near to paying a yet dearer price during the War, for the result was virtually to paralyse whole departments of government.

For Marxist theorists, another problem was appearing. Lenin had been quite explicit that, when the class enemies were finally liquidated, the machinery of government would wither away. In fact, it seemed to be obtruding upon private life more than ever. In 1936, Stalin explained that, while Communism prevailed in only one country, the State must exist in order to protect the proletariat from foreign enemies. In 1940 he advanced a different theory, denying what he had claimed earlier, that class distinctions in Russia had been eliminated.

'The abolition of classes will be achieved not by extinguishing the class war but through its intensification; the State will wither away not through making the governmental power weak, but by strengthening it to the utmost.'*

Since the death of Stalin, discussion has been less inhibited though, while physical repression is not so much in evidence, publications which are out of favour may receive less than their full allocation of paper. And while the Communist boast is that, unlike the Western press, printing facilities are in the hands of the people, still authors who fail to reflect 'partiynost' (sympathy with the Party's outlook) are unlikely to find their works selected for publication.

It was announced at the Twenty-second Party Congress, in 1961, that a new constitution was in preparation, since the stage had now been reached where the Dictatorship of the Proletariat might shed its class characteristics and become 'the state of the entire people'. Public discussion of the subject has been permitted, within limits, though no one appears to have asked when the State might now be expected to wither. But the editor of an important legal periodical† suggested in February 1965 that steps could now be taken to offer electors a genuine choice between candidates at elections.

In 1958, new codes of criminal law and of procedure were introduced, emphasising the principle that no one should be punished without trial. But where the judiciary is consciously (and, in fairness, openly) selected for loyalty to the Communist Party, and a judge may be removed if he falls foul of the Party leaders, such provisions are no more likely to prevail at times of political purges than did a similar provision of 1922. In fact the government has for some years been encouraging a campaign for legality, and has allowed a measure of public discussion on law and administration. But it is hard to escape the conclusion that the fate of human rights in the Soviet Union rests upon the views prevailing at any time among the leadership.

Even although the withering of State institutions is delayed, it is felt that the public should now be prepared for the time when there will be nothing to restrain anti-social behaviour

* *Problems of Leninism*, 1940 edn.

† *Soviet State and Law.*

but the censure of workmates and neighbours. An important function of the courts, therefore, is to educate the public, and from time to time pronouncements made and sentences passed are less concerned with the merits of the case than with emphasising a particular campaign (against hooliganism, drunkenness, or industrial inefficiency). Members of the public, for their part, are encouraged to take an interest in such matters.

Thus since 1957, comrade courts have been reintroduced. These are informal tribunals of workmates who pass judgment upon such offences as persistent lateness or drunkenness. Similar tribunals exist in certain neighbourhood units, and hooliganism among young people has been met by the formation of 'People's Guards', consisting of law-abiding young people selected by the Communist Party. The undoubted benefits of this policy are somewhat tempered by the opportunities for petty spite and, more dangerously, by the evolution of a society where friends and neighbours are encouraged to hound the non-conformist, even in those activities where the law does not presume to inhibit him. Where those who fall foul of the authorities are likely already to be foul of their neighbours, public opinion offers little safeguard against tyranny.

For example, while there is normally no official policy of religious persecution, it is made clear that Communist doctrine is hostile to religion, and those who seek to demonstrate their loyalty to Communism may well do so by open contempt for churches, synagogues and mosques. Thus religious groups frequently encounter difficulties with petty officials who are establishing to their own satisfaction their proper respect for the establishment.

In the United Nations, the Soviet attitude on human rights has been curiously chauvinistic. Soviet delegates have agreed enthusiastically that they should be recognised, and that each country should give effect to them in its own legal system. But in the General Assembly debate which led to the acceptance of the Universal Declaration, the Soviet delegate expressed two reservations. First, he commented that the Article dealing with freedom to disseminate ideas failed to solve the problem, since it would permit the diffusion of dangerous ideas, while it did not guarantee that the workers should have access to printing presses for the free discussion of lofty and just ideas. He suggested instead a declaration that it is the inalienable right of every person freely to express and disseminate democratic views, and to combat Fascism. (Remembering the variety of definitions now current of such terms as 'democratic' and 'Fascism', such a declaration would guarantee the expression of those views of which the government approves.)

Secondly, he reiterated a position adopted by Soviet delegates in the preliminary discussions, that to make the Declaration binding in international law, or to establish machinery for enforcement, would constitute an unwarranted interference with national sovereignty.

'Yesterday', he said, 'we were told, and hints were made in respect of sovereignty, that it was a reactionary idea. . . . Propaganda against sovereignty is nothing but an ideological proposition for the political capitulation of one country to a more powerful country before the economic power of that other country.' This pronouncement scarcely accords with the ringing assertion of the Communist Manifesto: 'The working men have no country', but it is a view to which the Soviet Union has subsequently adhered.

Yet it would be unfair, in assessing Soviet Russia, to overlook two factors. First, Russia has no tradition of democracy in the Western sense and, until recently, the leaders of that country were men who, prior to 1917, had themselves suffered from repression by a dictatorial government. So tyranny breeds tyranny. Secondly, Communist theory regards 'civil and political' rights, as envisaged in the West, as necessarily a sham, since every government exists in the interest of a particular economic group, and is merely part of its machinery for repression.

Nkrumah's Ghana

Since Ghana became independent in 1957 she has been widely criticised for a system of government that became progressively more illiberal—a criticism proportionate to the expectations originally held for a country which possessed one of the finest civil services in Africa, one of the strongest economies, and which, it was thought, had been safely launched into parliamentary democracy.

Apart from the central question of the degree to which individual rights were eroded, it is necessary to ask whether the circumstances in which an African country rapidly moved from colonial rule to independence in the post-war years were not such as to make the development of some alternative to full parliamentary democracy either inevitable or preferable, and secondly, once the country has settled to its own rule, whether there were not certain guarantees—of strong, central administration, economic good management, and a reasonable, social deployment of the country's wealth—to be weighed against the losses of liberty. These questions will be considered very briefly in turn.

The last contested general election in Ghana was held in 1956. The Opposition parties won 33 of the 104 seats to the National Assembly, but by 1960 opposition to the ruling Convention People's Party (CPP) in the National Assembly had disintegrated. Twelve of the Opposition members had crossed over to the Government, three were detained, and one was in exile. In 1960, after a manipulated plebiscite on the new Constitution, Ghana adopted a presidential form of government, the powerful presidential office to be filled by Dr Kwame Nkrumah, founder and life chairman of the CPP, and formerly Prime Minister. It was announced that the size of the mandate no longer justified the holding of the elections that were then due. By January 1964 there were only seven Opposition M.P.s. Of the by-elections necessitated by the detention and exile of Opposition M.P.s, the last to be contested was in 1960. In January 1964 a second plebiscite formally established a one-party state. In June 1965 no one offered to stand against the nominated candidates of the CPP, and elections were again declared to be superfluous. The 198 nominated members were announced as returned unopposed. 'Yesterday was indeed a glorious day in Ghana's history,' declared the *Ghanaian Times*. The CPP parliamentary party had forfeited its claim to be representative of the people.

The measure that did the greatest direct damage to the Parliamentary Opposition was the Preventive Detention Act of 1958, which authorises the President to order the detention of any citizen of Ghana 'if satisfied that the order is necessary to prevent that person's acting in a manner prejudicial to the defence of Ghana, the relations of Ghana with other countries or the security of the State'. It could be imposed for five years, renewable for a further period of five years. Applications for habeas corpus were not granted, since the illegality of the detention could be established only by demonstrating that the President was not in fact satisfied that the order he made was necessary, and the Courts found that the President was 'sole judge of his satisfaction'. There is therefore no appeal. In 1964 the system was extended by empowering the President to make restriction orders, involving certain described conditions of surveillance and control, where detention would not be suitable 'on account of age or health or for any other reason'.

The Universities were left free to operate without government interference until the beginning of 1964, when six senior members of Ghana University were deported, and a number of arrests made, including that of the President and other officers of the Ghana Students Union. The first arrests were followed by a rowdy and destructive procession of Party loyalists through the University compound. At the same time it was announced that scholarships awarded for courses at Ghanaian University institutions would be reviewed annually 'on the basis of satisfactory performance and good conduct', and the *Ghanaian Times* explained that . . . 'the hall-mark of good conduct should be close identification with the spirit and objects of the Party'. Lest anyone should be unaware of what these were, in September of the same year it was announced that all students entering the universities would in future have to do a two-week 'orientation' course at the Kwame Nkrumah Ideological Institute.

Press censorship was introduced in 1960, and was quickly used against the *Ashanti Pioneer*, a newspaper that supported the Opposition. News leaving the country was censored, and the radio was closely controlled by the Government. In

November 1964 the Government established a committee of nine persons under the chairmanship of the head of the Philosophy Department of Ghana University, empowered it to inspect bookshops, and the libraries of schools and universities, and instructed it 'to work out a system to ensure the removal of all publications which do not reflect the ideology of the party or are antagonistic to its ideals'.

The system was highly authoritarian. Apart from his powers of detention, and his control over the Judiciary, which is illustrated in a later chapter, Nkrumah was life chairman of the only legal political party and, as President of the Republic, was Commander-in-Chief of the armed forces, had the power of appointment, dismissal and 'disciplinary control' over members of the public services, and had discretion to grant loans out of any public fund 'if he thinks it expedient'. He could dissolve the Assembly and veto its legislation. Any person who, with intent to bring the President into hatred, ridicule or contempt, published any defamatory or insulting matter, whether by writing, print, word of mouth or in any other manner, was liable to imprisonment for up to three years.

All institutions were brought within the control of the CPP. Indeed it was largely the establishment of Party men as regional and district commissioners to administer the regions (and incidentally the polls) which undermined the Opposition in the country in the years immediately following Independence. Strikes were illegal under the 1958 Industrial Relations Act. In his famous Dawn Broadcast to the nation in April 1961, which first publicly revealed divisions within the CPP, Nkrumah had this to say: 'Coming to the integral organisation of the Party I consider it essential to emphasise once more that the Trades Union Congress, the United Ghana Farmers' Council, the National Co-operative Council, and the National Council of Ghana Women are integral parts of the Convention People's Party, and the Central Committee has decided that separate membership cards (i.e. separate to the party membership card) of the integral organisation shall be abolished.'

There are several reasons why one-party rule should have developed in Ghana. First, there never was a national party which offered any serious challenge to the CPP. Five Opposition parties shared the seats that the CPP failed to win in both the 1954 and the 1956 General Elections, and no one of these won as many as the other four together. At the time of the 1954 election, Nkrumah is reported to have said, 'Until Independence there is only one political platform—that is Independence—and I happen to be occupying it.' He was occupying it because he had outbid the moderate, intellectual leaders of the old United Gold Coast Convention, whose pace was too slow for a new and excited generation.

What the CPP had to contend with were parties organised on a regional basis—of which the most successful were the Northern People's Party and the Ashanti-based National Liberation Movement—whose quarrel with the CPP was not over legislative policy, but over the whole question of their integration into a unitary state. The NLM demanded the institution of a federal system. But federation would have been an expensive administrative regression; and it was precisely what the CPP, with its leaders' professed devotion to a 'socialist reorganisation' of Ghanaian society, was almost constructed to oppose. After all, it had an enormous majority of popular support throughout the country. The maintenance of national unity was a test of the competence of African self-government.

There really were no grounds to argue from the successful experiences of Anglo-Saxon parliamentary democracy, with its established conventions, its ancient habits and its great areas of self-restraint determining a character of political behaviour within agreed constitutional boundaries, to an uncreated state whose very character and constitution were the points at issue. The 'failure' of Ghana was very largely a fault in the logic of liberal expectations.

And the Opposition was not only, to the centralists, definitionally unconstitutional; it was also violent. In the days of the NLM it had been dangerous for CPP men to enter Ashanti. The press was always extravagant. To the CPP, their leader was 'Kwame Nkrumah, Man of Destiny, Star of Africa, Great Leader of Street Boys, Deliverer of Ghana...'. To the

NLM, 'If there is any notorious liar in this country whose word should never, never, never be trusted that man is Kwame Nkrumah. . .'. To the NLM, the CPP was the 'Communists' People's Party' and a band of 'thieves, rogues, traitors, double-tongued receivers of bribes. . .'.

Before the 1956 elections the CPP challenged the NLM to answer whether they would assume the role of a loyal opposition if defeated in the elections. The NLM replied: 'If we lose this election . . . it . . . would be a national disaster, and we . . . are prepared to meet it as such and to take all steps IN and OUT of the Legislative Assembly to mitigate the evil.'

The overwhelming victory of the CPP in the 1956 election killed the issue of federation. But there always remained the danger of secessionist revolt. Shortly after Independence there was rioting in the Ewe Togoland area, and the formation of a new tribal party—the Ga Standfast Association—that spread into Nkrumah's own constituency in Accra. The government produced the first of their repressive measures, the Avoidance of Discrimination Act, which forbade the existence of parties on a regional, tribal or religious basis.

Undoubtedly one of the unsettling features of these years was the rash readiness with which the Opposition leaders assumed any cause embarrassing to the government, however sectional or secessionary. J. B. Danquah, one of the old leaders of the intellectual opposition, later to die in prison, sat on the platform when the Ga party publicly and formally denounced Nkrumah. In 1958 an amateurish, half-formed plot to stage a *coup d'état* was uncovered. By late 1962 random acts of terrorism had become a commonplace. But by then two other factors had long since determined the course of governmental development. One was the untempered exhilaration of the CPP in its new position of power, which it all too readily accepted was there to be used to the utmost.

At the time of the 1960 plebiscite the Party newspaper pronounced: 'Our opponents and traducers should be reduced to a really abject situation . . . Whoever ranges himself against the CPP and Comrade Nkrumah will soon discover to his bitter chagrin that he is a mere butterfly on the great wheel of our party machine whose velocity is terrific.'

The CPP had once represented the country's will, and by that token considered itself entitled to the claim for ever; no other party could have a right to exist. In 1960 it was said that the CPP was 'more than a political party'; it was 'the living embodiment of the whole glory of our lives'. And the other factor was the personality of Nkrumah himself.

Nkrumah was a brilliant political organiser, an impulsive man with a romantic and personal attitude to power, and a professed Marxist. He was highly impatient of criticism, and at times carried his belief in 'colonial conspirators' beyond the point of ordinary political misinterpretation to the edge of hysteria.

His Marxism was individual enough for him to profess its compatibility with religion, to deny the existence of a class struggle in Africa, and to argue that the achievement of socialist ends does not require a physical revolution. His relations with Communism were always determined by the overriding requirement that Africa must remain internationally non-aligned and doctrinally individual. Nkrumah was capable of perfectly realistic political action, and his appreciation of the usefulness of Western capital, and of the strong tradition of Ghanaian private enterprise, was probably responsible for the fact that his Marxist ambition for the State ownership of the means of production went little further than the establishment of twenty to thirty unprofitable State corporations.

Nkrumah must bear a heavy share of responsibility for imposing a restrictive rule on what would otherwise have been a more open and competitive society. Until deportation and detention began to teach them their lesson, the original members of the CPP were strident, adulatory and naïve. A more tolerant leader, or one more respectful of human freedom, might have composed them, and the state they were forming, into a gentler mould. But both doctrine and temperament carried Nkrumah in his creation of a centralised unitary State beyond what seemed to be necessary to ensure integration.

Doctrinally, he wished to impose a centralised socialist State against what he knew to be indigenous resistant elements, and to use Ghana as a base to extend a single mass party over the entire continent of Africa. "Socialism" was what mattered: an independent judiciary was simply irrelevant. Temperamentally, he could rarely tolerate either criticism or reverse, and it is largely his unnecessary public acts of anger or spite that gave his government a bad name. It was a matter of unnecessary excess. For by ballot-rigging, by cruel treatment of individuals, and by voting himself rapid increments of power, he obscured both the enormous popular support which he and his party would always have won, and the very real threats to the State's existence that he could claim proper credit for overcoming.

How viable the State was, it was always difficult to guess. The civil service's competence had been reduced by the infiltration of Party men, and the departure of senior officials for a more congenial climate. Dismissals weakened both the police and the army. But only a crisis could test the strength of the administration. Single-party states tend to be rigid: they are institutionally insensitive to changing circumstances. And by eliminating the prospect of a change in power from within the constitution, the risk accumulates that the State collapses when power ultimately passes.

In the preface to his autobiography, Nkrumah had this to say: 'Capitalism is too complicated a system for a newly independent nation. Hence the need for a socialist society. But even a system based on social justice and a democratic constitution may need backing up, during the period following independence, by emergency measures of a totalitarian kind.'

But the institutions of a more just, generous and, in the long run, more efficient system were allowed to atrophy to the point where they would be useless to a generation that might prefer them, and the dangers inherent in the establishing of a unitary state yielded place to the dangers inherent in the continuance of an authoritarian rule. It was to be hoped that Nkrumah would permit a relaxation of the harsh totalitarian control that he had himself argued need only be temporary. But he failed to do so, and he was overthrown.

The Nkrumah regime was not as repressive as some other recently independent African states. Order was maintained and there was little loss of life due to violence. But it had deteriorated into a capricious and increasingly damaging autocracy; it had lasted too long; it was time for him to go, and he went without public lament.

The cruelties and waste of Nkrumah's regime, while appreciated, were certainly underestimated. Names and numbers of those detained ceased to be published; no independent investigation of prison conditions was permitted. Few people would have dared to conclude with confidence that the suggested number of detainees ran beyond the hundreds. It was obvious there had been wasteful expenditure on State corporations, on prestige projects, on overseas embassies, that latterly inflation had become uncontrollable—in all circumstances a political provocaton.

But the succeeding regime at once exposed, and began the attempt to redress, excesses that had been concealed. Soon 2,000 detainees had been released. The foreign exchange position was found to be desperate: the country was being financed by expensive and inefficient suppliers' credits, and even they were likely to dry up through default in repayment; there were no official currency reserves at all.

The new regime immediately succeeded in obtaining substantial foreign loans on soft terms, including £13 million from the IMF. By the end of June, 1966, a 40 per cent cut in expenditure in foreign embassies would already save £1 million a year in foreign exchange. The National Liberation Council announced they would return unprofitable State enterprises to the private sector, and negotiations have proceeded. Prestige projects—costing millions—have been suspended.

Internationally, the new regime has set about opening the doors that Nkrumah closed. There have been official opening ceremonies at the frontiers with Togo, Ivory Coast and Upper Volta. There will be no more subversive training camps.

All this will be economically helpful. Yet the two years, for which the military have said they will govern, will be critical, and for reasons largely beyond their control.

The Republic of South Africa

The story of South Africa is the story of a religion which has failed to cast out fear, and a fear which has become a religion.

The group of Dutchmen sent to the Cape in 1652 by the Dutch East India Comany found themselves surrounded by a dark-skinned people who resented the intrusion into their grazing grounds, and there arose between the two races a suspicion natural enough in the conditions. The attitude of the Afrikaner people has changed little from the outlook which they then acquired.

To this apprehension of the non-European, subsequent events have added the suspicion of Dutchmen for English-speakers, and of farmers for industrialists. And there has resulted a way of life which has constantly to assert itself, to convince itself of its own superiority, and in which race, language and religion have perpetually to be safeguarded from a threatening universe.

The end of the Boer War in 1902 found many leaders on both sides prepared to bury past bitterness, but there remained those who were determined to preserve Afrikanerdom from contamination either by native African or by Britisher. In 1914 they formed the Nationalist Party, with a twin platform of segregation of black from white, and of neutrality as between Britain and Germany. Between the Wars, the Nationalist Party became identified with the philosophy of 'Christian Nationalism', which borrowed much from that of Nazi Germany. It emphasised the destiny of the Afrikaner people as a nation superior to the races around them, and the importance of preserving its purity. It was anti-Communist and anti-Semitic. In 1948, Dr Diederichs, now a cabinet minister, expressed it succinctly.

'What is at issue is two outlooks on life. . . . On the one hand we have nationalism, which believes in the existence, in the necessary existence, of distinct peoples, distinct languages, nations, and cultures, and which regards the fact of the existence of these peoples and these cultures as the basis of its conduct. On the other hand we have liberalism, and the basis of its political struggle is the individual with his so-called rights and liberties. . . . This doctrine of liberalism that stands for equal rights for all civilised human beings . . . is almost the same as the ideal of communism.'

In 1942 Mr Vorster, then an official of Ossewa Brandwag, an organisation founded to perpetuate 'the spirit of the ox-wagon', and now Prime Minister, was even more forthright.

'We stand for Christian Nationalism which is an ally of National Socialism. You can call this anti-democratic principle dictatorship if you wish. In Italy it is called Fascism, in Germany German National Socialism, and in South Africa Christian Nationalism.'

After a split which led to the formation of the United Party, the extreme wing, still calling itself the Nationalist Party, was returned to power in 1948. It won the election on a minority of votes cast, but at once set about entrenching itself, and in the process implementing its programme. Since the Native Land Act of 1913, areas had been set aside as 'reserves' for occupation by Africans, and since 1923 there had been a policy of confining Africans in towns to specified parts set aside for them. In 1945 the Governor-General had been empowered to require any local authority to evict Africans 'in excess of reasonable labour requirements', and no African had been permitted to take up residence in a town without permission of a magistrate.

The Nationalists lost little time. In 1950 the Group Areas Act empowered the Governor-General to allocate areas to each of the three racial groups (White, African, and 'Coloured') and to confine them there. Thus the Government was entitled to uproot whole communities and remove them from contact with other races. Meanwhile, segregation within the cities proceeded. The Native Laws Amendment Act, 1952, forbade an African even to visit a town for longer than seventy-two hours unless he had the necessary residence qualification and was employed there. If he had no work he was no longer in a position to look for any.

Most hated of all the restrictions was the system of pass

laws. These imposed upon Africans the obligation to carry various documents, particularly those evidencing their right to be in an urban area. Without producing a pass or other necessary document an African could not obtain employment, pick up a pension or collect a parcel from the post office. Failure to carry a pass might lead to arrest, and to a fine or imprisonment. And it must be produced when demanded, for no time was allowed to go home and collect it. The curiously named Natives (Abolition of Passes and Co-ordination of Documents) Act, 1952, replaced these documents by a single reference book, which has pages for recording every aspect of the African's existence. The Act extended the requirement to women, and to many men who had previously been exempt.

Meanwhile segregation proceeded, where it did not already exist, in every other field. Natives were confined to types of work allocated to them by the Minister of Labour, and in 1953 it became an offence for Africans to strike. Segregation was rigidly enforced in the educational system, and no secret was made of the fact that much more expensive facilities were devoted to the education of Europeans than of Africans or 'Coloureds'. In the debate on the Bantu Education Act, 1953, Dr Verwoerd expressed the Government's objects frankly.

'What is the use of teaching the Bantu child mathematics if it cannot use it in practice? Education must train and teach people in accordance to the sphere in which they live. Good racial relations cannot exist where education is given under the control of people who create wrong expectations on the part of the native himself.'

But systematic racial discrimination requires some method of determining a person's race. So in 1950 the Nationalists were led to pass the Population Registration Act, requiring the entire population to be registered according to their race. Registration determines a person's entire legal status. The problem of classifying people according to race, as though no mixed breeding were possible and all the secrets of lovers were disclosed, had taxed the officials of Nazi Germany. The dangers were pointed out during the debate by General Smuts.

'I think all this probing into private affairs, this listening to informers, this effort to classify what is unclassifiable, what is impossible to achieve, will create a situation which will hit this country hard in years to come.' The Director of Census need give no reason for his decision, and a fruitful field of gossip has been provided for spiteful neighbours and business competitors.

Not unnaturally, legislation of this kind has ensured that a free election, at which all races were enfranchised, would offer the Nationalist Party little prospect of retaining power. Already before 1948 Africans were denied the vote everywhere except in the Cape and Natal. Even there, the African and coloured franchise, unlike that of white people, was subject to effective educational and property qualifications, and African and coloured women had no vote.

In 1951 the government introduced a bill to remove coloured voters from the electoral roll in the Cape, and substitute a separate electoral roll, which would return four (white) representatives. The bill having been passed in the manner required for ordinary legislation, it was declared by the Appellate Division of the Supreme Court to be invalid, since it was contrary to an 'entrenched' provision of the South Africa Act, and could therefore be effected only by securing a majority of both Houses in joint session. Almost the kindest epithet applied to the Court by any cabinet minister was 'a bunch of liberals'. The government then secured the passing of a bill providing that Parliament might review any judgment of the Appellate Division declaring legislation invalid. Parliament proceeded to reverse the decision of the Appellate Division. This Act, and the consequent 'judgment' of Parliament were at once declared invalid by the Supreme Court.

During the controversy, Dr Malan resigned as Prime Minister, and was replaced by Mr Strijdom, who brought with him a reputation as a strong man. He piloted through Parliament an Act raising the necessary Quorum in the Appellate Division to eleven, and appointed five new judges to that Division. He also introduced successfully a bill to enlarge the Senate from forty-eight to eighty-nine. At a joint session of the two houses he then secured the passing of the South Africa Constitution Amendment Act, which debarred any court from inquiring into the validity of any law other than one dealing with language rights. He also steered through the original bill providing for separate representation of coloured voters. At about this time the Government began a policy of appointing to the Bench lawyers who were thought to be more amenable to its views.

The Nationalist Party had professed from early days to stand guard against the menace of Communism. It quickly began to apply the word to all its opponents. An attempt to outlaw all anti-Nationalist organisations in 1950 produced such a public protest that the government withdrew it, replacing it by the Suppression of Communism Bill, which was duly passed. The Act empowered the Governor-General to declare unlawful any organisation which professed or promoted Communism, or which engaged in activities calculated to further the doctrine. The officials of such an organisation, and those taking part in its activities, or contributing to its funds, were declared guilty of an offence punishable by up to ten years' imprisonment.

The definition of 'Communism' set out in the Act is considerably wider than anything to be found in the writings of Marx. It includes 'any doctrine or scheme which aims at bringing about any political, industrial, social or economic change within the Union by the promotion of disturbance or disorder, by unlawful acts or omissions or by the threat of such acts or omissions or by means which include the promotion of disturbance or disorder, or such acts or omissions or threat...'. The Suppression of Communism Amendment Act, 1951, carries the definition further. 'Communist' is there defined to mean 'a person who professes or has at any time... professed to be a Communist or who, after having been given a reasonable opportunity of making such representation as he may consider necessary, is deemed by the Governor-General... to be a Communist'. Thus, as Mr Gerald Gardiner, Q.C., now Lord Gardiner, the Lord Chancellor, remarked, 'If you were a Communist forty years ago, you are a Communist today. And whether you are a Communist or not, you are a Communist if the Governor-General says that you are'.

The Act also empowered the Government to prohibit the printing, publishing or distribution of any publication expressing Communist views. Already since 1939 the importation of large numbers of books had been forbidden under the Customs Act, which prohibited the import of goods which are 'indecent or obscene or on any ground whatsoever objectionable'. Under the Act of 1950 the Government has banned a number of periodicals. And the Publications and Entertainments Act, 1963, now empowers the Government, through its Publication Board, to ban any newspaper, book, film or stage show, or work of art.

By 1951, therefore, a large section of the Government's potential opponents, amounting in fact to about four-fifths of the population, were already disenfranchised, and their right to criticise publicly had now likewise been taken from them. The United Party still functioned, but since it differed from the Nationalists in degree of moderation rather than in the direction of its policies, it hardly provided an outlet for their views. Not surprisingly, such organisations as the African National Congress began to express their disapproval in the form of mass demonstrations. In June 1952 there was launched a campaign of non-violent disobedience to certain segregation by-laws, curfew restrictions and pass regulations. Over 8,000 protesters went to prison. The Government decided to take stricter measures against demonstrators. The Criminal Laws Amendment Act, 1953, made it an offence to break any law by way of protest or as part of a campaign. The punishment provided was a fine of £300 or three years' imprisonment, or ten lashes, or all three. Anyone inciting others to do so was made liable to heavier punishment.

By this time, too, every meeting of any suspect organisation was attended by members of the Special Branch of the police, equipped with notebooks, and in consequence of decisions by the courts limiting their right to attend private meetings, a provision in an Act of 1955 empowered policemen to attend private meetings.

In March 1960, a peaceful anti-pass-law campaign led to the killing by machine-gun fire from the police of six people at Langa, a suburb of Cape Town, and sixty-one at Sharpeville, a suburb of Vereeniging. Many others were injured, and the scene at Sharpeville after the shooting was described by one eye-witness as 'like a battlefield'. A number of children were among the casualties. The Government responded by declaring a state of emergency and assuming virtually limitless powers of detention without trial. By the end of April 4,500 Africans were under arrest. Shortly afterwards legislation was passed indemnifying the authorities against all claims for compensation arising out of the incidents.

The Unlawful Organisations Act, 1960, empowered the Governor-General to ban the African National Congress and the Pan Africanist Congress, which he proceeded to do, thus driving them underground. By now the resistance movement had no alternative but to disband or proceed by illegal methods. The General Law Amendment Act (the 'Sabotage Act'), 1962, imposed penalties ranging from a minimum of five years' imprisonment to the death penalty for sabotage, and anyone merely found trespassing might be required to prove that it was not for the purpose of sabotage. The Minister of Justice was empowered to subject to house arrest anyone who in his opinion was furthering the objects of Communism, or to prohibit him from performing any class of act.

By March 1963, 154 persons had been prohibited from attending public gatherings, many of them avowed anti-Communists. The International Commission of Jurists commented that this Act reduced the liberty of the citizen to a degree unsurpassed in any dictatorship.

In 1963 a further General Law Amendment Act completed the pattern. It provides that when a person is serving a sentence under the Suppression of Communism Act, the Sabotage Act, or certain other statutes, and the Minister of Justice is satisfied that he is likely to advocate or encourage any of the objects of Communism, he may be kept in gaol indefinitely after the expiry of his sentence. The Act also provides penalties, including a death sentence, for persons who have furthered the objects of Communism with the assistance of a foreign power, or have undergone training to further the objects of an illegal organisation, since 1950, that is, for activities carried on up to thirteen years before it was passed. It gives wide powers of arrest and detention without trial for up to ninety days at a time, entry upon private premises without warrant, and opening of private mail. There is considerable evidence that persons detained under the ninety-day provision have been subjected to solitary confinement, electric shock treatment, and torture, to obtain information about their associates.

In seventeen years South Africa has become a police state emulating in many respects the model adopted by its present leaders before and during the War. Dr Verwoerd's conception of his own destiny was expressed in his first broadcast after becoming Prime Minister.

'In accordance with His Will, it was determined who should assume the leadership of the government in this new period of the life of the people of South Africa.' He later told a reporter, 'No, I do not have the nagging doubt of ever wondering whether, perhaps, I am wrong'.

This attitude is expected to pervade the whole administration. In October 1961, Senator de Klerk, Minister of the Interior, told the Public Servants' Association:

'We must decide as State officials in which direction we are going, French or German. Do we in the first place wish to serve the public, give public service, be employees in the service of the public and be badgered by the public, or are we officials of the State, giving service to the State?

'If we do not wish to be public servants but State officials who give service to the State and maintain law and order in the name of the State, with the State President at the head of affairs, then we must not seek to identify ourselves with our fellow mortal, as is done in the United Kingdom, or, as in France, seek to serve the public.'

South Africa has the distinction of having probably been condemned internationally for infringements of human rights since the War more often than any other country. At the 1961 Prime Ministers' Conference, the pressure from other members of the British Commonwealth to expel South Africa was only forestalled by that country's herself resigning membership. In the debates preceding the acceptance of the Universal Declaration, South African delegates insisted that such a declaration should deal only with the most fundamental rights. They argued, for example, that human dignity was not infringed by telling a person that he could not reside in a particular area.

Since then, South Africa has shown herself indifferent to repeated resolutions of censure, and frequently the only countries voting with her have been Portugal, France, Spain and, unhappily, the United Kingdom. On occasion even these have felt unable to support her.

A Committee appointed by the United Nations Security Council to consider technical problems relating to economic sanctions has tended to become linked in discussion with the question of South Africa's defiance of the United Nations in relation to her usurpation of authority in the South-West African territories. It is possible that, after all, South Africa may one day transpire to have rendered a great service to the cause of human rights by compelling the whole civilised world to join in a practical programme of enforcement.

Portugal

For the fifteen years following the overthrow of the monarchy in 1910, Portugal had a rapid turnover of ministries, accumulating inflation, and a depreciating currency. An unmanageable situation was brought to an end by a military *coup d'état* in 1926. In 1928 Dr Salazar accepted the Ministry of Finance from General Carmona. He was a competent accountant and an obdurate personality. Within a year he had eliminated a £3,000,000 budgetary deficit by a ruthless retrenchment of Government expenditure. By 1932 he was Prime Minister. In 1933 the Constitution of the 'New State' was promulgated.

The Constitution would at first sight seem to guarantee certain liberties. In the terms of Article 8, 'the rights and individual guarantees of Portuguese citizens' include 'liberty and inviolability of religious beliefs and practices', 'the free expression of thought in any form', 'freedom of teaching', 'freedom of meeting and association'.

But entitlement to these constitutional rights is thereafter qualified. In paragraph 2 of the same article it is stated that 'special laws shall govern the exercise of freedom of expression of opinion, education, meeting and association. . . . They shall prevent, by precautionary or restrictive measures, the perversion of public opinion'. The obligation on the State to have regard to the unspecified claims of morality is widely emphasised. In Article 6, 'It is the duty of the State to promote the unity, and establish the juridical order, of the nation by defining and enforcing respect for the rights and guarantees of morality, justice or the law'. In Article 14, 'with the object of protecting the family it is the duty of the State and local bodies to take all measures necessary to prevent the corruption of morals'.

And so on. In default of any appointed arbiter between these 'moral requirements' in a given situation, and the claims of individual liberty as stated in Article 8, these qualifying cautions become a discretion reserved to the Government to be as liberal or restrictive as it dares or pleases, within the blessing of a permissive constitution.

In two other respects is the Constitution demonstrably illiberal. First, there are some liberties that it declines to recognise. Strikes are illegal, by Articles 26 and 39. And in paragraph 3 of Article 8, imprisonment without formal charge is permitted for a range of stated crimes, from wilful homicide, burglary, and larceny, fraud or embezzlement 'when perpetrated by an habitual criminal' to 'crimes against the State'.

Secondly, and more importantly: it prescribes a political organisation whose resemblance to democracy is very tenuous indeed. There is a National Assembly 'elected by direct vote of the electors for four years', but neither the President, who is Head of State, nor the Ministers are responsible to it. The President appoints the Prime Minister, who is responsible to him, and the cabinet ministers are appointed by, and are responsible to, the Prime Minister. Article 112 of the Constitution is very explicit: 'The Government depends exclusively upon possessing the confidence of the President of the Republic, and its continuance in office shall not depend upon the fate of its draft bills, nor upon any vote of the National Assembly'. Moreover, under Article 109, it is the duty of the government to draw up decree-laws, and these decree-laws do not require to be ratified by the National Assembly if published during the nine months of the year when the Assembly is not specified to sit.

But periodic elections are specified for the National Assembly and, more importantly in view of the limited powers of that body, for the office of President. In practice there has been one inversion of the powers as assigned under the Constitution, and Dr Salazar, who has never submitted himself to an election, has controlled the Presidency by securing the candidature and return of his own nominees. Nevertheless, the President has the formal power of dismissal over the Prime Minister. How have these elections operated?

Qualifications required at law restrict the range of the electorate. Men must be literate, and pay a certain minimum in taxes; women, in addition, must show a certain level of secondary or technical education. Voters must make a personal application to join the voting register, and provide proof of the necessary qualifications. However, the administration reserves a mere arbitrary power, and 'all persons professing opinions contrary to social discipline and the independence of the State' are also ineligible for a vote, interpretation being exercised by the administration's agents. So a rough attempt can be made to restrict the poll to those likely to support official candidates. In the 1961 National Assembly elections, of all those who had attained their legal majority only 25 per cent were entered on the electoral registers.

But electoral prejudice is not confined to electoral law. In the case of all candidates for the National Assembly or the Presidency the government reserves a right of approval. Of political parties, only one—the National Union—has a legal existence; canvassing, correspondence, the distribution of pamphlets and manifestoes, the holding of meetings in any other name than that of the National Union, are illegal and render those responsible liable to arrest. Opposition candidates are allowed no access to the electoral register, on which to base their contact with voters. The government not only refuses to distribute the lists of opposition candidates to voters (the voter is responsible for bringing to the poll the list of candidates he is voting for), but have made the paper on which the official list is printed of a special quality, with the result that it is evident to party officials at the polling-booth how individuals are voting. At the count itself, the government has consistently refused to allow any representative of the opposition to be present.

In the face of such difficulties, it is not surprising that in twenty-five years only twice in elections to the National Assembly have any opposition candidates stood against the official list. In 1965 the opposition candidates, as has become customary, withdrew in protest at the conditions of contest. As far as the Presidential elections are concerned, the rules, restrictions and history have been the same. In 1947 Norton de Matos, ex-ambassador to London, withdrew on the ground that no fair election was possible. In 1951, on the death of President Carmona, Professor R. L. Gomes, a distinguished mathematician, was disqualified by the government, and Admiral Meireles withdrew for the same reason as Norton de Matos.

But in 1958 a serving officer, General Delgado, contested the Presidential election through to the end. His chances were injured by each of the above restrictions; in addition he was prevented from attending meetings, his canvassers were arrested, his electoral lists intercepted, and for the six weeks over the election his leading protagonists were arrested and detained. After the election, in which he had declared his intention of dismissing the Prime Minister if returned, he was himself dismissed from his post as Director-General of Civil Aviation and relieved of his army commission. The result of the poll, as announced, a 3–1 victory for the official candidate, was hardly interesting. But the excitement of the campaign had been disruptive.

Later in the year, an electoral college for the election of the President was substituted for direct suffrage. Composed of members of the National Assembly—already once politically sifted—and of various nominees, its establishment removed the last hope of popular influence in the composition of the political citadel.

The government does not confine the repression of dissidence to the control of elections. Censorship of the press was introduced in 1926. The Censorship Service can act against any publication which 'might induce the public to error', and can prevent the entry into Portugal of any foreign publication 'containing matter the disclosure of which would not be permitted in Portuguese publications'. There are further controls on the expression of opinion. Under another early Decree-Law, 'Officials or employers, civil or military, who have shown or show a spirit of opposition to the fundamental principles of the Political Constitution, or who do not guarantee to co-operate in achieving the higher aims of the State, will be suspended or retired, if they have a right to this, or if not will be dismissed'. And lest it be thought that only the government has a duty to notice disaffection, another Decree-Law of 1936 threatens with suspension, retirement or dismissal, heads of departments 'if any of their respective officials or employees subscribe to subversive doctrines, and it is ascertained that they did not use their authority or did not inform their superiors'.

In Portugal the State has some structural control in the professions, and lawyers, doctors, and teachers are subject to these legal conditions. Each Civil Servant before taking up a post must swear an oath that he or she is 'a loyal member of the social order established by the Political Constitution of 1933' and 'actively opposed to Communism and all subversive ideas'.

Freedom of Association is a stated constitutional liberty, but trade unions are illegal, political parties are illegal, and all associations must provide the civil authorities with copies of their rules, lists of their members and officers, and any other information demanded. All associations carrying out their activities wholly or in part in secret are illegal; imprisonment is prescribed for all ordinary members of such associations, on discovery, and 'increased sentences' for their officers.

The principal agents of arraignment are the Political Police —the PIDE—and the sanctions are applied by the Special Courts and the Political Police themselves. There are two Courts, in Lisbon and Oporto, which were set up in 1945 with special judges for the trial of political cases, and they sit continuously. The sentences of the Court are stiff: for comments injurious to the President or Prime Minister up to two years' imprisonment; for taking part in a strike up to eight years; for 'lowering the prestige of Portugal abroad' from two to eight years.

Distinct from their ordinary powers of sentence—a maximum for each crime being provided in law—the Courts can apply 'security measures', that is to say they can sentence to imprisonment for an unspecified time, according to a view of a person's potential 'danger to society', and unrelated to the establishment of his guilt for any crime he may have committed. These 'security measures' will be applied to persons convicted of an offence, to be served by them after the expiry of their ordinary sentence, or to persons in respect of whom a charge is brought, but not proceeded with. In both cases imprisonment as a 'security measure' is to be served for a maximum of three years, extendable 'by successive periods of three years as long as they continue to show themselves dangerous'.

Strictly, this is equivalent to life imprisonment, being imprisonment for a time never specified in advance and indefinitely extendable at the discretion of the executive; and, life imprisonment being prohibited under the Constitution, this forms one of the few Government practices the constitutional legality of which can be challenged.

The PIDE are a virtually sovereign body. They have powers to ban meetings and gatherings, to enter and search any residence, and to close 'places which . . . may be used by their owners to facilitate subversive activities'. They have power to arrest without warrant whomever they choose to arrest. They have power to imprison without charge for six months. They may imprison, release, and re-arrest without ever preferring a charge, indefinitely. It is their duty to scrutinise the civil servants, voters, teachers, and candidates for political unorthodoxy. It is they who recommend to the Special Courts the suspension or extension of the 'security measures'. They are the sole judges of the necessity for their actions, against which there is no appeal.

The interrogation and treatment of detainees by the PIDE and in the prisons have been the source of much anxiety, and of periodic requests for investigation. In 1957 two such requests were made following the trial of fifty-two young persons in Oporto, and the death of two people in the PIDE prison: one by seventy-two lawyers of Lisbon and Oporto, the other by thirty-three lawyers of Coimbra, of all political views, and including the Deputy Civil Governor and the President of the Town Council. All of them had been impressed by the evidence of brutal treatment. The Government threatened some of the lawyers with 'security measures': but they conducted no enquiry.

In August 1965 the Portuguese Ambassador in Washington, in a letter to the *New York Times*, justified his régime in these terms: 'It should not be surprising to fair-minded persons that the Portuguese people prefer continuity in Portugal . . . as such continuity will guarantee to them . . . order in the streets, economic development with no foreign assistance, financial stability . . . and the maintenance of Portugal in the anti-Communist camp. All this they have enjoyed with the present political régime . . .'.

What the Portuguese prefer may not be thought a matter which the authorities have taken pains to discover. Continuity of government has been provided, but that, indeed, is largely the point at issue. Economically, adherence for three decades to the deflationary policy that cured the crisis of the late 1920s —a policy made possible by unemployment and the repression of strikes and the trade unions—has indeed ensured stable prices and a stable currency. And the degree of prosperity which Portugal has attained as a result is not impressive.

She has a dollar income per head no more than one-sixth that of Sweden, and one-quarter that of the United Kingdom; her consumption of energy per head is one-twelfth that of the United Kingdom, her infant mortality rate four times as high as the United Kingdom, and UNESCO found that for 1950 her illiteracy rate was 44 per cent as against a rate of 3–4 per cent for France, and 1–2 per cent for West Germany. There is large-scale unemployment, with consequently a heavy net emigration. Social security benefits are minimal.

Politically, the government claims that all its harsh measures are justified by the menace of Communism: and one of the logical results of this is that the PIDE spend much of their time in trying to make plausible examples of Communism out of the individuals in their hands—through the extraction of confessions, etc. A more sophisticated consequence is that the government develops an actual interest in the continuance of a controllable measure of Communist activity, and it is at least arguable that the uninterrupted operation of illegal Communist printing presses within the country owes more to the connivance, than to the inefficiency, of the Political Police.

In any event the government has never intended to confine its repression to Communists and Communist activity, as the extracts from the laws quoted above are sufficient to indicate. In May 1961, before the General Election, the leaders of the liberal opposition issued a lengthy document entitled 'Programme for the Democratisation of the Republic'. Among other things, it demanded the restoration of civil liberties, the reform of the electoral law, the disbandment of the Political Police, and adherence by Portugal to the principles of the United Nations Charter. It was immediately denounced by the government as an attack on 'the moral unity of the nation' and the Public Prosecutor ordered the institution of proceedings against the sixty signatories to the Programme.

General Delgado was certainly no Communist; he was vilified by the Communist Party during the earlier part of the 1958 Presidential election, and was initially opposed by a rival candidate of the Left whom the Communists supported.

In 1959 the Bishop of Oporto was exiled from Portugal. In July 1965 the government again refused to give permission for the formation of a Christian Democrat Party as it has repeatedly refused the same application in the past.

And there is another result of government policy. So much pressure in the end compresses all opposition into the same harness. Towards the end of the 1958 Presidential campaign the Communist candidate stood down, and the Communist Party gave its support to General Delgado. Now the Government could say Delgado was Communist-backed! The Communist Party provides the only focal point of well-organised opposition to all who would play some active part of protest or revolt against the present government. One day it may make revolutionaries of enough milder-mannered men for it to accomplish its mission.

4
Theory and Practice

The United Kingdom

. . . the issue
Involving principle but bound in fact
To squander principle in panic and self-deception—
Accessories after the act . . .
Louis MacNeice: *Autumn Journal VII*

WHEN THE responsible elements in a society have sent a man to prison, it is likely that they already have a grievance against him. And if there is any doubt whether he has been properly imprisoned, they will probably reiterate the fact in order to convince themselves that he has merely met with his deserts. Thus they will work themselves and their subordinates into a passion of hatred against him, for there is no better material for hating a man than the possibility that you may have wronged him. And while the government will not normally condone actual violence, those officials who are in daily contact with him may be less restrained. Particularly is this so if, seeking to justify the imprisonment to the public and (it may be hoped) to their own conscience, the authorities demand from him a confession. Persuading him to admit what they are (by now) sure that he had done, they are frequently tempted to employ more than moral persuasion.

This chapter is a study of a situation where no such brutality was planned. The tragedy was brought about not by wicked men, but by men who never stopped to consider it possible that they might be wrong.

Prior to independence, Kenya was administered under the authority of the United Kingdom Government by men trained in British standards. Its affairs were not worse conducted than those of most colonial territories. But by 1952 economic grievances and political repressions had produced resentment among Africans. The form which it took was only partly political. The frustration fermented against a background of tension between the old tribal society and the new way of life; between the pagan religions and the teachings of Christian missionaries. And the injustices against which the African community complained were identified in the minds of many with the breakdown of the old religion and the old society. Like others who at various times have revolted against injustice, they spoke of the good old days and determined to set back the clock.

Among the Kikuyu, the movement took a revolting form. Mau Mau groups were formed, pledged to defend the old ways against the European. Those who joined underwent an initiation ceremony accompanied by oaths of loyalty to the movement and enmity to the white man. At first they were simply the old tribal oaths, but in time the Mau Mau developed forms of their own, accompanied by the killing of cats, sexual practices and even ritual murder. The initiates regarded these oaths as binding to a degree where their actions could hardly be said to be voluntary. Mau Mau held the Kikuyu villages in terror. Villagers who refused to co-operate were murdered. White men were murdered as a matter of course. If attempts were made to bring the killers to justice, witnesses were murdered. The bodies of some were never found. On occasion whole communities were murdered—men, women and children.

From 1952 to 1954 Kenya was a land of horror. It may be argued that a different policy in the 1940s may have produced a happier result, but undoubtedly the Kenya government was faced with an emergency. And no legitimate criticism can be advanced against the introduction of emergency regulations. The drastic nature of the surgery must be judged with reference to the disease. On 24 April 1954 Operation 'Anvil' was launched. Over the next few months, 35,000 members of the Kikuyu, Embu and Meru tribes were detained. By September 1955 15,000 Mau Mau members had been convicted of criminal offences and were imprisoned. But over three times that number of people were in custody without having been tried. They had been convicted of no offence, but officials had decided in each case that they may have been associated in some way with Mau Mau. And since the terrorisation of witnesses rendered it difficult in many cases to obtain convictions, there is little doubt that many guilty men would have remained at large had there been no detention without trial.

Between April 1954 and Septtmber 1955 Mau Mau was broken, and it may be argued that the emergency measures had proved to be justified. Three problems remained—to catch and convict the remaining members of the movement who had committed crimes, to ensure that there was no spreading of Mau Mau ideas from the pockets where they held out, and so far as possible to eradicate these ideas from the minds of those in custody who had been infected. This was no light undertaking, for psychologically many of them were obsessed with the oaths which they had taken. The rehabilitation began.

The authorities held the view that the best antidote was to make the detainees work, under supervision, until they had become re-accustomed to the disciplines of social co-existence and co-operation. And so far as possible they were then to be encouraged to confess their association, since some of them believed that confession broke the power of their Mau Mau oaths. For the purpose of arranging the programme of work, they were taken to special detention camps. The treatment was as effective as any mass conversion under such difficulties was likely to be, perhaps surprisingly so. By the end of 1956 the number of Mau Mau convicts still detained had been reduced to 7,780. But there were still 30,000 detained unconvicted, on the view of the authorities that it would be unsafe to release them.

It was decided to try a further method of rehabilitation which was officially labelled 'dilution'. The hard cases were to be split up, and to mingle with those of their own race who were co-operating and prepared to work. So far as possible, they were to be removed from the environment in which they had maintained their resistance to authority, and it was hoped that, before they had settled down in their new camps, they would find themselves among groups who were actually working. Immediately upon arrival they were to be stripped of any objects having Mau Mau associations, like amulets, and even beards. Thus they would be caught unawares, and the barrier penetrated.

Between the end of 1956 and 1959 the programme of salvation by works continued. Those Kikuyu whose loyalty to the government was not in question, and who were employed as warders, had a particularly difficult time. They were looked upon by the more intractable detainees as traitors to their people, and even those of their own tribe who were not influenced by Mau Mau ideas may have displayed some feeling that such active support for the authorities showed an indifference to African nationalism. The European officers had a relatively unrewarding task, as year succeeded year in the intense heat and dust. Normally, the camps were in the least populated, and therefore the least attractive, parts of Kenya.

Reports began to circulate of violence among detainees, of riots, and the killing of warders. Similarly, complaints by prisoners of bad treatment began to emerge from the camps. Some of them were undoubtedly exaggerated, and some entirely without foundation. But some were clearly well founded. In 1957 one Machiri, son of Githuma, died of cerebral haemorrhage. The magistrate who conducted the inquest found that he had been suspended from a beam by his wrists and beaten with strips of rubber. After being cut down, he was suspended again and the treatment repeated.

At Aguthi camp, Kabugi, son of Njuma, died shortly after his arrival at the camp. Two other detainees were taken to hospital. At the inquest, the coroner was told by the acting officer in charge that while working, Kabugi had 'complained that his legs were not working properly. He was told to stop work.' The finding of the inquest was death from natural causes. Letters smuggled out of the camp to Mrs Barbara Castle, M.P., suggested that this was not the truth of the matter. A question in the House, and subsequently an anonymous letter to the Secretary of State, resulted in further investigation. It transpired that death had resulted from an over-zealous attempt to extract a confession. Detainees had been taken upon arrival to a roundabout. They were compelled to run around it in the oppressive heat. They were then taken to a football field, where they had to carry buckets of soil on their heads until they confessed their Mau Mau activities. They were not permitted to enter the camp until they had confessed. Kabugi refused to confess, and was forced to continue carrying buckets of soil until he collapsed and died. So, at least, was the finding of the Court which tried the African warder Githu. For Githu, whose official title was a 'rehabilitation assistant', was charged with committing 'actual bodily harm'.

In 1957 a delegation from the International Committee of the Red Cross visited the camps and reported that they were satisfied. From one camp there was subsequently a report by prisoners that signs of ill-treatment had been deliberately concealed before their arrival, though the allegation cannot be regarded as proved. There was also an investigation by Mr Heaton, a British prison official, who expressed himself as reasonably satisfied.

By the beginning of 1959, those who had been detained at the beginning of Operation 'Anvil' had been in custody for over four-and-a-half years. Some, who had been detained even earlier, had been kept from their normal lives and their families for six-and-a-half years. On 24 February 1959 the Opposition moved in the House of Commons for a Parliamentary enquiry, and the Government quoted the number of Mau Mau convicts still in custody as 4,000, while 2,400 were still detained without trial.

The camp at Hola was divided into three parts. In the settlement were a number of detainees with their families, cultivating plots of land and living a life as close to normal as their continued detention permitted. The open camp contained those who were not appropriate for the settlement, but who were not regarded as desperate. The closed camp was inhabited by those whom the authorities regarded as the hard core, and whose rehabilitation had virtually not begun. In the closed camp were 208 detainees.

A further consignment was expected soon from another camp and it was felt that if a mental breakthrough was possible at all, it should be attempted before the newcomers arrived. Mr Cowan, a senior prison officer with a distinguished record, was sent to Hola. He arrived, conferred with the Governor, and suggested a plan. Its essence was that the recalcitrants should be divided into four groups, which should be taken out one at a time and compelled to work. The second group would be brought out only when the first was working. When both were working, the third should be brought out, and so on until all were working. The procedure was to be the same in the case of each group. Mr Cowan subsequently said that he anticipated that they would work when required to do so under these conditions. The prisoners were men who had consistently refused to work, and there appears to have been no reason why they should now co-operate, but Mr Cowan had had considerable experience in dealing with such prisoners, and his expectation may have been based upon his knowledge of their psychology. However, the plan provided that, should they refuse to work, they were to be 'manhandled to the site of work and forced to carry out the task'.

These words have acquired a wealth of interpretation comparable with the better-known passages of the Bible. Mr Cowan subsequently explained: 'I meant that their arms would be worked—put through the motions for the task and compelled to carry out the task.' The prospect of working a man's arms by superior strength, with the object of seeing who gets tired first, may be sufficient to discourage such an interpretation by any official. The magistrate who subsequently conducted the inquest declared that 'any reasonable person would consider (the words) as *carte blanche* to use whatever force might prove necessary'. He found that there was a 'complete absence of direction with regard to the amount of force which might be used'.

There has been considerable argument, too, as to the degree of force which could lawfully have been authorised by the government, under existing legislation. Undoubtedly, prison officers were entitled to use reasonable force in suppressing violence. And senior officers were entitled, as a disciplinary measure, to order up to twelve strokes with a light cane. It seems clear that there was no authority to order beating with any heavier implement purely as a punishment. Indeed, if any legislation had authorised it, the legislation itself might be open to criticism.

The Cowan Plan was approved by Mr Lewis, the Commissioner of Prisons. But in practice a number of difficulties presented themselves. Owing to illness, a large proportion of the prison staff were off duty, and there were not nearly as many available as had been envisaged. Consequently, the arrangement to divide the prisoners into four groups was abandoned. Instead of applying the plan to sixty-six prisoners, divided into four groups, it was applied to eighty-five in a single group. Mr Cowan had intended the work to be performed without tools. The work was in fact digging a trench, and it was decided that tools would have to be used.

Mr Sullivan, the Commandant, told the authorities that he was in difficulties. He was ordered to proceed with the plan. He asked for a copy of the plan. None was supplied. He asked for a senior officer, with summary powers of punishment. None arrived. Whatever the merits of the plan as originally conceived, Mr Lewis agreed at the inquest that the arrangements actually made constituted 'in effect, a different plan'.

The prisoners were taken out and ordered to work. The Askari warders in charge had short batons, and other warders, from the riot squad, had larger ones. Mr Sullivan had ordered that they should be beaten if they 'made trouble'. On the way a number of prisoners set up a 'Mau Mau howl' and threw themselves on the ground. There is no suggestion that they were violent, although the warders may have thought mistakenly that they were attempting to escape. Others, when put through the motions of working, resisted the warders who were compelling them. But throughout the operation, only one warder was injured, and it did not subsequently emerge how his injury was sustained. Yet for reasons which are still confused, the prisoners were beaten with batons, until eleven were dead.

No telephone was available, but a wireless message was sent, and since it was not known whether mutiny had broken out, three officials, headed by the Deputy Commissioner of Prisons, arrived quickly at the Camp. They were there for three hours. What they were told, and by whom, has never clearly emerged, but their report was to the effect that 'because of the gap of three hours between the last scuffle and the first death, it was the opinion of all with whom we spoke that the compelling exercise was in no way connected with the cause of death'. In addition to the content of this report, the word 'scuffle' is a curious one in view of the facts subsequently ascertained, since it does not appear that there was any aggressive violence on the part of the prisoners except, in a few isolated cases, to escape being put through the motions of work.

After the report had been considered by the Governor, a press hand-out was given on the following day. It stated: 'The deaths occurred after they had drunk water from a water cart which was used by all members of the working party and by their guards.' (This was literally true.) There is no evidence that any particular official was responsible for suppressing the facts. At which point they were suppressed has never appeared. At the inquest the Coroner found it 'impossible to understand how Mr Campbell could properly report that "there was no apparent evidence of punitive beating"'. And as the Secretary of State subsequently pointed out in the House of Commons, it was virtually certain from the moment when the deaths occurred that the truth would emerge. But that someone had been less than frank seems an inevitable conclusion.

There was a disciplinary enquiry, where Mr Sullivan was charged, together with his assistants, with gross dereliction of duty, in:

(a) putting eighty-five detainees to work without ensuring that there was proper supervision, and contrary to the Cowan plan;

(b) failing adequately to superintend the operation;

(c) failing to prevent warders in his presence from improperly assaulting detainees.

He was retired, but without loss of gratuity, since it was found that he did not deliberately disregard his instructions. Mr Lewis retired at his own request. In the June Honours List, Mr Cowan was awarded the M.B.E.

The purpose of this chapter is not to apportion blame, but to point the lessons that emerge. The most obvious seems to be that violence ought not to be inflicted upon prisoners who are not themselves offering violence. If it is used, it should be strictly in accordance with regulations permitted by law and set out (in writing) in detail. Officials who are given imprecise instructions are susceptible to errors of judgment in the best of conditions, and in the heat and tension of Hola the probabilities of mistakes were substantial.

The danger of such incidents is increased when an emergency operation is prolonged. The emergency in Kenya was real enough. It may be questioned whether emergency measures continued to be justified after so many years. And when a government decides that circumstances justify detaining people without trial—people, that is, who may be innocent of any offence—there is a particular responsibility to ensure that they are not ill-treated.

When men are detained without trial, it is always tempting for the authorities to extract confessions if they can. The detention is thereby shown to be justified. When to this inducement there is added a theory that confession is good for the soul, and it becomes declared policy to encourage confessions, the danger is magnified. A man who may be innocent should not be subjected to ill-treatment for refusing to confess his guilt.

The United States

Must then a Christ perish in torment in every age to save those that have no imagination?

George Bernard Shaw: *St Joan*

The United States is proud of its record as the land of rugged individualism. It is hailed as the land where people from widely differing backgrounds may each express their own culture and way of life, and where success is determined by individual ability. But even so broad and tolerant a society is subject to occasional waves of hysteria, in the course of which nothing short of complete conformity is tolerated.

In his thirties, William K. Sherwood was a rising man whose success was proportionate to the social value of his work. He had been a brilliant science student, graduating with First Class Honours at Chicago and Washington. He had broadened his academic field by a period at Oxford, studying the social sciences. Now he was engaged on cancer research at Stanford University. He was studying for a doctorate in biochemistry, and in the written examination had obtained the highest rating in his group. He was happily married, with four children.

But there is some reason to believe that, at the age of twenty-two, he had taken part in a Communist discussion group. Even earlier, he had helped to organise medical supplies for the anti-Franco forces in the Spanish Civil War. However, this had been investigated by the FBI in 1942, and he had been cleared of 'security risk'.

Early in 1957 he was visited by agents of the FBI. The connection of one Bill Sherwood with a Communist study group in 1938 had been recollected in 1955 by a witness at a hearing of the House Un-American Activities Committee, in Chicago. The Committee ('HUAC') had itself a curious history.

The House of Representatives and the Senate, like the Houses of Parliament in Britain, have power from time to time to set up committees, charged with the task of investigating a particular problem. This is because a necessary incident of the power to legislate is the right to investigate the facts which indicate what legislation is necessary.

Although the United States Constitution prohibits Congress from usurping the function of the courts, it is sometimes convenient for Congressional committees to adopt a procedure similar to that employed by the courts. Thus they summon witnesses, who are required to give evidence on oath. In 1857 a Statute provided that to refuse information demanded by either House was to be a criminal offence, punishable by imprisonment for up to one year. Proceedings under the Statute would be brought in the ordinary criminal courts and, although the Houses continued themselves to punish for contempt where they thought fit, it has now become customary to bring proceedings under the Statute.

During the 1930s, when the New Deal legislation was formulated, Congress made considerable use of the investigation procedure to discover facts concerning monopolies, financial manipulations, and political graft. And it was at this time that politicians and press alike realised that, in addition to providing information, investigations could prove to be of first-rate news value. Exposures emerged which monopolised the headlines, and public opinion could become fiercely hostile to some of the witnesses whose activities were exposed. While liberal politicians urged a vigorous use of the procedure, the more conservative elements declared in the strongest terms that it was undemocratic and contrary to the Rule of Law.

Not until after the War did the political Right discover that it might use the instrument for its own purposes. In 1938 a committee was set up to investigate 'un-American' activities, and some members and witnesses seized the opportunity to label supporters of the New Deal as Communists. In 1945 this Committee was added, rather as an afterthought, to the list of permanent House of Representatives committees. Immediately, the Committee made it its mission to expose Communists and Communist sympathisers. In 1947 an investigation into the motion picture industry purported to show that Hollywood was riddled with Communism, and for weeks the nation spoke of little else. The Representatives who formed the Committee became popular heroes almost overnight, and a number of senators quickly sought to attract similar publicity by introducing the same type of Communist-hunting into Senate committees. In 1946 the Senate had established a permanent Investigatory Sub-Committee, which later became the Permanent Sub-Committee on Investigations of the Committee on Government Operations. Its later history has become indissolubly associated with the name of Senator Joseph McCarthy. And other Congressional committees, like the Senate Sub-Committee on Internal Security, provided publicity for aspiring anti-Communists.

The irony of politics confronted the liberal elements with the weapon which they had helped to forge. And jurists like Mr Justice Frankfurter, who a generation earlier had observed that Congress could be trusted not to abuse the power of fact-finding necessary to its legislative function, began to express doubts. For the questions asked, and the comments of the committees, were directed less and less to any possible legislation, and concerned themselves almost exclusively with attacking political opponents. This was brought about partly by the necessity for convincing the public that the administration was riddled with Communist conspirators, bent upon overthrowing the Constitution, and that the safety of the nation depended upon the continuation of these investigations.

A proposal to change the Constitution was itself conclusive evidence of a desire to bring America under Russian domination. But there is little doubt that the committee members proved to be their own most ardent converts, for they persuaded themselves into a frame of mind in which punishing an individual for past or present Communist activities became an object in itself.

The pattern of Congressional investigations is now fairly clear. The Committee selected its target (a government department, a university, an organisation, or an industry), and announced that it had evidence showing Communist activities in those circles on such a scale as to create a national danger. The press publicised the announcement under sensational headlines. Counsel to the Committee and his staff collected a number of witnesses anxious to co-operate (often professional *agents provocateurs*) who, in due course, gave evidence that they had once associated, or pretended to associate, with Communist circles, and could produce lists of people who were concerned in those activities.

Those listed might then be called upon, and told that if they confessed publicly to their activities, and in turn named their ex-associates, they would themselves be treated as friendly witnesses. This meant that they would be given special seats at the hearing, and publicised as loyal Americans. If they refused, they were nevertheless issued with subpoenas to attend and rigorously cross-examined by counsel to the Committee.

Normally, the first question asked was: 'Are you now or have you ever been a Communist?' And sometimes a witness declined to answer. He was then liable to be prosecuted and imprisoned under the Statute of 1857, unless he could urge some reason why he should be excused from answering. He might object that his private views were not the concern of Congress or the press, and invoke the First Amendment to the Constitution, which provides that Congress may make no law abridging freedom of speech or the press. There seems no doubt that this provision prohibits the use of investigating committees to curtail freedom of speech.

But a witness may be compelled to answer the question whether he has ever been a Communist, and to identify others involved in political activities, if the House of Congress has authorised an enquiry to which the question is relevant, and the aim is justified on balancing individual freedom against governmental security. As the Communist Party's intention is 'the ultimate overthrow of the Government of the United States by force and violence', the power to investigate its activities is a wide one. A number of witnesses have been imprisoned for insisting on their view of the First Amendment, and refusing to answer the questions of Congressional committees.

Another safeguard available to Americans under the Constitution is the provision contained in the Fifth Amendment, that no person shall be compelled in any criminal case to be a witness against himself. The provision has been construed more widely than the words suggest, to mean that no one is bound to incriminate himself as to any charge which may form the subject of criminal proceedings, and this, indeed, is the approach of English Common Law. The Supreme Court has ruled that questions relating to membership of the Communist Party, and any part played in its activities, may give rise to incriminating answers, since the witness may be liable to prosecution under the Smith Act.

It has been reiterated again and again, both in America and the United Kingdom, that if the privilege against self-incrimination is to have any effect, guilt must not be implied from silence. But this has not been the view of Congressional investigation.

'Well, now,' Senator McCarthy explained to a witness, 'you have told us that you will not tell us whether you are a member of the Communist Party today or not, on the ground that if you told us the answer might incriminate you. That is normally taken by this Committee and the country as a whole to mean that you are a member of the Party, because if you were not you would simply say "No", and it would not incriminate you.... Therefore, you should know considerable about the Communist movement, I assume?'

Hence anyone invoking the right guaranteed to him by the Constitution is likely to be branded 'a Fifth Amendment Communist', a phrase probably originating from McCarthy, but later in general use.

A witness who answers a question without objection is deemed to waive the privilege, not only in relation to that question, but to any others relating to the details of the matter. (Otherwise he might choose to answer only questions which help his case.) A favourite manœuvre of McCarthy was to ask a witness whether he had ever engaged in Communist espionage. If he replied 'No', the Senator would claim that he had waived the Fifth Amendment 'insofar as the field of espionage is concerned'. The rule has been described by Mr Justice Black as making the protection 'depend on timing so refined that lawyers, let alone laymen, will have difficulty in knowing when to claim it'. In consequence, witnesses who wish to protect themselves against having to answer questions about their entire associations, or disclose details of others who may have expressed sympathy with Communism years ago, were frequently led to claim the Fifth Amendment when asked the first question.

It was not unusual for a witness who claimed the privilege to find himself asked a long series of related questions, to each of which it was known that he would plead the Fifth Amendment. The press were then invited to report that he had pleaded the Fifth Amendment sixty-seven times. And frequently enquiries degenerated into a search for witnesses who were likely to invoke the privilege, so that an imposing tally of Fifth Amendment objections might be reported.

Those cited to appear before investigation committees were in jeopardy of widespread publicity, involving social ostracism and the loss of their employment. Such, indeed, was the avowed object of many investigations. Questions like 'Have you discussed with your employers your appearance here today?' were frequent, and witnesses were asked to state publicly the names and addresses of their employers, when their only purpose could be to ensure that the publicity resulted in dismissal. Exposure was often followed by physical violence. One Congressman, informed that hearings conducted by him had been followed by victims being dragged forcibly from their jobs, commented: 'This is the best kind of reaction there could have been to our hearings.'

It might have been thought that investigations attended with such consequences would be conducted with every safeguard for the innocent. In fact witnesses were subjected to abuse from committee members and from counsel, unless, of course, they were friendly witnesses. And in reply, their only right was to answer questions. They must not 'make a speech', and if they intervened during the abuse, they might be silenced with the comment: 'There is no question pending.'

A witness was entitled to have a lawyer present, but the lawyer's right was merely to advise his client. He might not address the Committee, or speak for him. And he ran the risk of himself being branded as a Communist. Witnesses have been asked, 'What did your counsel just advise you?' or even, 'How long have you known your counsel?' and 'Do you know your counsel in any capacity other than the capacity of attorney and client?'

What transpired between the FBI and William Sherwood is not known, but it seems probable from the experiences of others visited at about the same time that he was pressed to name those with whom he had been associated in the study group, nearly twenty years earlier. He was visited three times, and there seems little doubt that he refused to give the information demanded.

In June 1957 HUAC was to descend upon San Francisco to conduct an investigation into Communist 'intellectual infiltration' on the west coast. About a month before the hearing, Sherwood received a subpoena to attend. He wrote to the Committee requesting a postponement of his own examination for three days, in order to read a scientific paper at a conference in Vancouver. His letter may not have been tactfully worded, since it was reported that he commented on the subpoena that 'it causes me to lose precious time from work which is of importance to humanity'. The postponement was refused. (His paper was subsequently read by someone else, and was highly regarded.)

As the date for his attendance approached, Sherwood became increasingly depressed. The effects of a public appearance upon his career and his social life were likely to be disastrous and permanent. When he heard that the hearings were to be televised, his anxiety increased. He told his wife that he was 'going to end it all', but while she, too, was worried, she did not take him seriously. Late at night on 16 June, he went to his laboratory, and there he killed himself by poison.

He left a letter, saying: 'In two days I will be assassinated by publicity . . . I would love to spend the next few years in laboratories, and I would hate to spend them in jail.' (The reference to jail refers almost certainly to proceedings for refusal to answer questions.) He left a statement for the Committee, in which he declared that its 'trail is strewn with blasted lives, the wreckage of useful careers'.

The Committee chairman, Congressman Walter, expressed 'disappointment'. He said that the death was 'unfortunate' because the Committee had reason to believe that they could have obtained useful information from Sherwood.

Already there had been signs of public revulsion against the excesses of the investigating committees. The death of Sherwood brought home to large sections of the American public the effects of the witch hunt. And there seems now to be widespread agreement with a pronouncement of Mr Justice Douglas who, reviewing the case of a conductor on the New York underground, dismissed as a security risk, commented: 'Total security is possible only in a totalitarian régime—the kind of system we profess to combat.'

But even in May 1965 HUAC was still busy in Chicago, publicising evidence from friendly witnesses to suggest that the Civil Rights movement in the South was infiltrated by Communists. The names of eleven people subpoenaed to attend before the Committee were leaked to the press before the hearings, and there was little evidence of a change of heart on the part of the Committee. The difference between 1965 and 1957 consisted in the volume of public protest, and even public demonstrations. The hysteria which threatened to change the American people into a national lynch-mob has subsided. But there remain those who might seize the first opportunity to re-create it. And no change in the political climate can restore the career and the life of William Sherwood.

The Soviet Union

What is the knocking?
What is the knocking at the door in the night?
It is somebody wants to do us harm.

D. H. Lawrence

Politicians, even those with little interest in the arts, like to believe themselves responsible for a flowering of cultural activity. Their problem is that art cannot be delivered to order, or its production figures included in planning statistics. It is helpful, of course, if economic assistance is available where it is needed, but little of value is likely to emerge unless artists are free to produce what they feel to be worth while. And sometimes the results are not what the authorities had in mind.

In his earlier years, Valeriy Tarsis might have been designed for the Revolutionary government of Russia; a gifted author who was, by background and inclination, a sincere Communist. He was born in Kiev in 1906, only a year after his father had actively assisted the revolutionaries of 1905, and had fortunately remained undetected by the authorities.

Other members of his family were busy in the Revolutionary movement. When the revolutionaries themselves became the government, they could support the régime with conviction, and as a young man Valeriy joined the Communist Party. From 1929, when he graduated at the University of Rostov, until 1937, he was an editor in a State publishing house. He wrote in his spare time, and published two short stories, a study of contemporary Western writers, and a number of translations into Russian.

It may not have been Valeriy Tarsis who changed. More probably it was the régime. But certainly, by the period of the terror, in 1937, he was no longer an enthusiastic supporter. His support became no warmer when, in the 1940s, his father was included in the number of pre-Revolutionary Communists who disappeared permanently under Stalin. Nevertheless, there could be no complaint of his war record.

He became a war correspondent, with the rank of captain. At Stalingrad he took part in the fighting, and was twice seriously wounded. It was while he was recovering that he met Olga Alksnis, and later married her. Her uncle had been a general who was shot during the terror in 1937.

The character of Tarsis's writing changed. He wrote novels and short stories, which became increasingly critical of the régime, and he developed a biting satirical style. It is a boast of the Soviet Union that there exists there a freedom of the press which is denied in the West, since there the printing presses and publishing facilities are controlled by the people, and are not monopolised by the 'ruling class'. But Tarsis was to learn that the publishing houses which in fact controlled them were certainly no less conformist in their selection than their counterparts elsewhere. The writings which he submitted were constantly rejected, year after year. The death of Stalin was undoubtedly followed by a more liberal period, when writers were led to believe that they might express themselves frankly, but Tarsis, who was among those to respond, found that the permitted limits, though wider, were as effectively enforced as ever. After repeated disappointments, it was borne upon him that, if he wrote as he believed, there was no prospect of having his work published in Russia without a major change in the climate. And for that there was no reason to hope.

By 1960 he had a collection of manuscripts which seemed destined to remain unread. What finally drove him beyond the Rubicon is not clear, but in that year he left the Communist Party, resigned from the Union of Soviet Writers, thus virtually sealing himself off from any prospect of publishing in Russia, and sent his manuscripts abroad. They contained probably the most outspoken writing to emerge from Russia since the Revolution. Western publishers were interested. In 1962, two of his stories were published under the title *The Bluebottle*.

They were studies of the condition of writers under the Soviet régime. Typically Russian in their irony, their satire was described by one reviewer as 'biting, bitter, passionate, yet tragic, with something of the quality of Dostoyevsky, of Gogol too'.* The English translation was followed by others.

Even before publication, Tarsis made no effort to conceal the fact that he had sent his manuscripts abroad. What follows is taken from his subsequent novel, *Ward 7*, described as 'an autobiographical novel'. The central character is Valentine Almazov, a writer who allowed it to become known that he had sent his manuscripts abroad. Tarsis describes how, shortly afterwards, Almazov received a telephone call from the secretary of his Party committee, inviting him to 'drop in tomorrow at noon, Valentine. Let's talk it over. We'll do our very best to help you.' He called at the time suggested, and was introduced to 'some comrades from State Security'. The two secret police agents warned him that, if he failed to recall the manuscripts, he would be in serious trouble.

It was too late for compromise. He wrote to Khrushchev, asking permission to go abroad. For some months there was no answer. The answer came when he was visited one evening by 'two policemen, the head janitor who, like all head janitors, was employed by the police, and a nosy woman who, according to the head janitor, represented the "community" destined in future to replace the organs of the State'. He was taken to the police station, from there by ambulance to the chief city psychiatrist, and thence to a mental hospital.

Although *Ward 7* does not purport to be a factual account, there is no reason to doubt that it provides a substantially accurate description, both of Tarsis's own experience, and of the people whom he met. Certainly, he was certified insane in August 1962, two months before 'The Bluebottle' was published.

Tarsis was not the first. This method of dealing with political opponents had been used in Russia before the Revolution. From 1917 until the death of Stalin there is little evidence of it, since a régime which employs labour camps, forced service in salt mines, and mass shootings has no need to resort to such devices. But after Stalin, the authorities

* Leonard Schapiro in the *New Statesman*.

sought to convince the world that political repression in Russia had ceased, and they appear to have been sincere in their wish for a more liberal system.

The difficulty was that, where two generations of officials have grown into habits of repression, two generations of writers have been deprived of serious discussion, and two generations of politicians have become accustomed, where the views of an individual have been inconvenient, to silence him as a matter of course, established ways of thinking inevitably push their way to the surface. Indeed, the public has become conditioned to respect conventional behaviour, and itself to accept responsibility for enforcing it, to the point where the unconventional, behaviour, appearance, or ideas, are regarded as both objectionable and dangerous. In any society, the division between the unconventional, the eccentric, and the insane must depend upon definitions imposed partly by public opinion, and partly by its expression in legal form. It may well be that for Soviet officials a failure to appreciate and publicise the benefits of life in contemporary Russia is conclusive evidence of insanity.

Certainly other writers since Stalin have met similar treatment. And stories have circulated of young men whose families have actually requested that they should be sent to mental hospitals when the alternative was political imprisonment. An intellectual in 'The Bluebottle' is warned that if he persists in writing unwelcome material he is in danger of being certified insane, 'in accordance with a well-established Russian custom', and it may be that even when that was written, Tarsis was concerned to warn the world that, if he was sent to a mental hospital, it should not be taken to reflect upon his sanity.

Section 39 of the Kanatchikov Hospital, where in the novel Almazov is incarcerated, contains 150 'patients', only one of whom is genuinely in need of mental treatment. Of the others, some are there because their political views made it necessary, or because they have drawn attention to themselves by writing to the authorities about what they considered to be political problems. Others had simply crossed the paths of Party officials, or their friends. The book speaks eloquently of the frustrations of those who are cut off from their families and their work, but there is no suggestion of serious ill-treatment. The opening sentence is: 'Perhaps for Valentine Almazov the worst was the slow, empty passing of time.'

In February 1963 the story of Valeriy Tarsis broke in the Western press. A month later he was released. For a period he was compelled to live off his friends, since he was no longer a member of the Union of Soviet Writers, and could earn nothing in Russia by his pen. But at last came permission to receive his foreign royalties. And by the summer of 1965 he was established as a centre of intellectual discussion in Moscow, and it was even possible privately to obtain one of the manuscripts of 'The Bluebottle' or of *Ward 7*, which circulated in the city.

Recollecting the outspoken content of *Ward 7*, which was even more forthright than 'The Bluebottle', there is reason to remark the great advance of Soviet Russia from the brutalities of the Stalin era. Tarsis expressed the view* that he was left free partly because the Soviet government is now sensitive to world opinion, and partly because the new men in the Kremlin, Khrushchev's successors, are uncertain how to react to criticism. Indeed, they may wish to see the development of genuine public discussion in Russia, but find that there lack both the institutional framework and the habits of thought within which it could take place.

Tarsis is not the last of the 'new Pasternaks'. On 6 October 1965 the *Guardian* carried a report from some British students who, on a visit to the Soviet Union in 1964, met a student interpreter, Zhenya Belov. During that visit he impressed them as an enthusiastic and well-informed supporter of the régime. On their second visit, in 1965, he was troubled about the absence of opportunities for discussion in 'the State of the whole people'. He had expressed his ideas at a meeting of his Party organisation, at the Moscow Foreign Languages Institute. The Party had reacted by suspending

* Interview reported in the *Evening Standard*, 11 June 1965.

him from membership. He wrote to the First Secretary and to the Prime Minister. On the return of the British students, some weeks later, Zhenya Belov had been taken to a mental hospital.

Perhaps the most important lesson suggested by recent events in the Soviet Union is that the road to tyranny is much quicker and easier than the way back.

Ghana

'I'll be judge, I'll be jury,' said cunning old Fury;
'I'll try the whole cause, and condemn you to death.'
Lewis Carroll: *Alice in Wonderland*

In August 1962 the first attack was made on the life of President Nkrumah. As he left his car in the small northern Ghanaian village of Kulungugu, a hand grenade exploded, killing those next to him and wounding many others. On 29 August Tawia Adamafio, Minister of Information, Coffie Crabbe, Executive Secretary of the CPP, and Ako Adjei, Minister of Foreign Affairs, were detained on grounds of their participation in the attempted assassination.

Under the Preventive Detention Act, Nkrumah had unchallengeable power to detain these men indefinitely. Instead, probably because he thought that there was enough evidence to secure a conviction, which would be both an example and a justification, he chose to put them, and others who had been arrested in connection with the same affair, on trial. In October 1961 the Criminal Procedure (Amendment) Act had been passed, to establish a Special Court which was to deal with offences against the safety of the State, such as treason, or offences against the peace, such as unlawful assembly, or offences 'specified by the President by legislative instrument'. The Special Court was constituted by the Chief Justice according to the request of the President, and there was no appeal against its decision. By legislative instrument, the President could make any 'necessary' adaptations to the Court's procedural code.

On the second reading of the Bill in the National Assembly, K. A. Gbedemah, the organisational genius of the CPP, who was removed from office when Adamafio and his followers were promoted, attacked it fiercely. The Ministers of the Interior asked rhetorically who could believe 'that Kwame Nkrumah who is so constitutional in all his deeds, so wise and kind as he always has been . . . could create a system of Court offensive to our motto, Freedom and Justice?' Gbedemah replied. 'If we are to learn from experience, this is a Bill which when passed into law would soon show that the liberty of the subject is extinguished for ever. . . . There is no appeal and hon. Members of the Parliament of Ghana are being asked to pass this Bill into law. Today, we may think that all is well, it is not my turn, it is my brother's turn, but your turn will come sooner than later.'

But Nkrumah was soon to learn that the findings of a court, even when it was one subject to so much executive control as this, are not always predictable.

In April 1963 seven people arrested after the Kulungugu attack were found guilty of treason by a Special Court, consisting of Sir Arku Korsah, the Chief Justice, and two judges of the Supreme Court. Five were sentenced to death, and two to terms of imprisonment. In August the Court resumed to hear the case against Adamafio, Coffie Crabbe, Ako Adjei, and two others, a government clerk and a former opposition Assembly member. On 9 December the two others were convicted, but Adamafio, Coffie Crabbe, and Ako Adjei were acquitted. No one who studied the evidence imagined that the verdict could have been otherwise. Nevertheless, on 11 December, Nkrumah dismissed Sir Arku Korsah from the office of Chief Justice, as he had power to do under the 1960 Constitution. On 23 November the National Assembly, in special session, passed the Law of Criminal Procedure (Amendment No. 2) Act, empowering the President to set aside any decisions of the Special Court. On 25 December Nkrumah duly declared the judgment null and void.

The dismissal of the Chief Justice delighted the *Ghanaian Times*. Sir Arku Korsah had 'failed in his duty, let his leader down and betrayed his country' by not telling Nkrumah beforehand what the verdict would be. State security, it was said, was essentially within the province of the President.

At the end of the year it was announced that a referendum would be held in January on two amendments to the Constitution. One would 'provide... that there will be one national party in Ghana and that the one national party shall be the Convention People's Party'; the other would 'invest the President with power in his discretion to dismiss a Judge of the High Court [as he had already power to do in the case of the Chief Justice] at any time for reasons which appear to him sufficient'. By a 'mixture of intimidation and ballot-rigging', in the words of two London correspondents who attended the trial, nearly three million votes in favour as against less than three thousand against, on a 93 per cent poll, were recorded to ensure the adoption of the amendments. Radio Accra explained its importance thus:

> 'If we were to continue on our course towards socialism, the Judiciary, as well as any other section of the State apparatus, had to be welded into the socialist administration. The judges had to be controlled by the people, not the other way round... At present a judge on appointment is far above the people and becomes an independent power. There will be no such entrenched offices and such privileged persons in the State when the people have voted "yes" for this referendum. When the referendum is over, the history of socialist Ghana will truly begin.'

The five men against whom the verdict had been annulled were kept in prison under the Preventive Detention Act until 24 October 1964, when a second trial on the same charges was opened against them before a reconstituted Special Court, consisting of a new Chief Justice, T. Sarhodde Addo, and, this time, of a jury. The jury was composed of Party members, some of whom were wearing in Court their Party smocks. After the first trial, Adamafio's counsel had been arrested and detained. At the second trial the defendants protested that they had been unable to get counsel to represent them, and they remained unrepresented throughout the trial.

On 9 February 1965 all five defendants were found guilty and sentenced to death. Six weeks later Nkrumah announced that he had decided to commute the sentences to twenty years' imprisonment.

The interest here lies more in its neat example of a country dispensing with its Judiciary than in the description of a substantial addition to the lost liberties of Nkrumah's Ghana. For personal liberties were really completely deprived by the Preventive Detention Act, an arbitrary and ugly Presidential instrument, designed for use in ordinary times of peace and unrestrained by any provision of appeal or reasonable limit on sentence.

Nkrumah's dismissal of Sir Arku Korsah was the impulsive, petulant act of an autocrat. Nor does it seem politically to have been very wise. For inevitable publicity has attracted an attention that many crueller, and equally unjustifiable, acts of detention have escaped. And the logical arabesques performed by the Party Press, and on occasion by the government, in explanation of these and other similar actions, only added to the infuriation of those whose particular concern is the freedom of the individual at law.

The International Commission of Jurists denounced the 'shocking sophistry' of the argument advanced in the 1951 Government White Paper to recommend the Preventive Detention Act, where it said that 'the letter of the law should not be enforced in all its severity. The execution of political prisoners is something which should only be done in the last resort. Preventive detention makes it possible to avoid exerting the full rigour of the law....'

It should not escape notice that in this case President Nkrumah commuted the death sentence. There has not been one political execution in Ghana, and this is an example for the rest of Africa. But the distressing feature of this history is the overt destruction of one of democracy's essential supporting institutions—an incorruptible Judiciary.

It is pleasing to record that the succeeding regime has shown every inclination to restore some independence to the Judiciary. A legal committee has been established to review the laws of the land which "encroached on the fundamental freedoms and welfare of the people of Ghana". The Preventive Detention Act has been repealed by Decree Law. In May 1966 the Act of 1963 that enabled Nkrumah to declare null and void the judgment given in the case that has been the subject of this chapter, was abolished. And judges are now only removable on the recommendations of the Judicial Services Commission. The institutions of justice have been given a new lease of life.

The Republic of South Africa

I was . . . sick, and in prison, and ye visited me not.
St Matthew's Gospel, Ch. 25

Ill-treatment of prisoners may arise from a variety of causes. It may be the result of a deliberate policy of cruelty, as in some Nazi concentration camps. It may be the result of public indignation against the prisoners, as when it takes the form of lynching. It may be due to an error of judgment in a difficult situation, when the problem is to prevent a repetition. Or it may arise from sheer indifference to the men and women who suffer.

In 1954 the Secretary of Native Affairs in South Africa issued a general circular setting out a scheme under which Africans arrested for certain technical offences, chiefly in connection with Pass Laws, need not be charged at once with the offence. Instead, they might be taken to the local employment officer, an official of the Department of Native Affairs. And he might offer them an alternative to being charged. They could instead take employment in certain rural areas. 'This scheme', it was explained, 'aims primarily at assisting unemployed natives to obtain employment.'

The scheme appeared to offer a merciful alternative to an appearance in court and probable imprisonment. With more detailed safeguards, and humanely administered, it might have operated in that way. But even an enlightened scheme may be dangerous if those to whom it is applied are persons of no consequence. Its actual method of operation appears from the story of James Sadika. This account is taken from a statement later given by the victim himself, and corroborated by numerous statements from others involved.

James Sadika was a qualified herbalist, living in Alexandria, a native suburb of Johannesburg. He was happily married, with two children. In October 1958 his wife took the children on a visit to relatives, and for a short period he was left alone.

Unfortunately, he mislaid his reference book. He applied at the Pass Office for a duplicate, duly paid his ten shillings, and was told to return in a fortnight. Meanwhile, he was given another document, but it is not now clear what it said. In due course he returned to the Pass Office, and was told that he should have paid five shillings for a permit. He explained that he did not know this, and offered the five shillings. It was now too late, he was told. The substitute document was of no interest to the official. He had committed an offence and would be sent to work on a farm for six months.

He was taken into custody, and detained from Friday until the following Tuesday. He was then taken by the police, with three other Africans, to the Farm Labour Bureau at Nigel, a rural area. The official in charge of the Bureau told them that they would wait for farmers who needed 'boys' to work for them. Although the scheme was clearly expressed to be optional, no one appears to have asked them whether they agreed to accept employment. Mr Sadika attempted to protest to the official, who struck him across the face, and told him that he had no choice. He and three others were then taken into an office. A document was placed before them, and they were ordered to place their thumb prints upon it. There is little doubt that this was a contract by which they 'voluntarily' agreed to serve a farmer for six months, at a wage of £3 per month. (Mr Sadika was previously earning between £10 and £15 per month.) They were warned that they could easily be identified by their thumb prints, and that if they escaped they would be caught and punished.

He was taken to work for a farmer. He does not say how he arrived at the farm, but there are statements from other Africans on this stage of their experiences. One (who was in a different group) tells how, having been selected by the same farmer, who chose the biggest, they were told that they must pay five shillings for a permit to work for him. Although he was not short of money, he had none with him at that time. The farmer announced that he would pay the money and deduct it from their wages.

Having arrived at the farm, Mr Sadika and the others were at once ordered into the fields to work. They worked under the supervision of 'boss boys', Africans who had been selected by the farmer as supervisors, and who enjoyed to the full their positions of authority. (Readers of *Uncle Tom's Cabin* will remember 'Sambo' and 'Quimbo'.) One of them, Philip, introduced himself by striking him on the head with a knobkerrie. He asked him for money, and Mr Sadika was relieved of the £2 12s. 6d. which he was carrying. Another, Abram, arrived too late to collect money, but he administered a beating and took his shoes, watch and pants. This seems to have been an experience to which all new arrivals were subjected.

After their work was finished for the day, they were allowed to drink water from an oil drum standing in the open air. Then they were locked for the night in their quarters. These were in a brick building containing a number of rooms. There was only one entrance, locked on the outside, and all the windows were barred. The workers were allocated to their rooms. In one, about forty-five of them slept. This was the big room for newcomers. Those who had been there longest were given the privilege of sleeping in one of the other two living-rooms, one containing about a dozen, and the other fewer. The building contained another, smaller room, which seems to have been used for the injured and the dead. There were a few beds, but most had to sleep on the cement floor.

Lavatory accommodation consisted of an oil drum, cut into two. The two halves were used by everyone, and remained in the building where they slept and ate. All the statements agree in describing the conditions as unimaginably filthy.

They were infested with vermin, and the sacks and blankets which served as bedding were never washed. They were bloodstained and bug-infested. None of the workers was ever permitted to bath or even wash. Since they were locked in the building from Saturday evening to Monday morning, they were able to sweep the scraps of food from the floor and place them in a bag, which was emptied once a week, on Sunday. But there was no opportunity to dispose of the lavatory tins from Friday until Monday.

Food consisted of porridge and coffee, three times a day. Sometimes it was hot. Sometimes it stank so that they could not eat it. Sunday was a special day. One piece of meat was added to each man's porridge. They were allowed to drink water from the drum before work started in the morning, and on returning in the evening. But frequently there was such a rush for water on their return that it would be used before some had drunk at all. None was available for washing.

Since most of them had lost their clothing to the boss boys, they wore sacks with arm holes. Beatings seem to have been regular. Sometimes they were administered to encourage the slower workers; sometimes to initiate new arrivals into the way of life. The farmer and his sons frequently saw the beatings, and sometimes took part in them. Blows were given with knobkerries or hoes. Hoes seem to have been used in particular to mutilate the feet of the workers, so that they could not run away. Mr Sadika was too badly crippled to think of escape. When a worker fainted, Philip would sometimes urinate into his mouth, as a method of reviving him.

One day Abram was striking out with his knobkerrie at workers who, he thought, were too slow. He struck one, a newcomer named John. He struck him on the back of the head, and John fell. Abram struck him again, but John remained where he had fallen. Abram called Philip, and they tried to lift him to his feet. It quickly became clear that efforts at revival were too late. John was dead. This was sufficiently unusual to interrupt normal routine. Other workers came to look. Philip explained that John had died from the heat. He told the workers to lift the body on to a trailer. They did so, and it was placed in the room reserved for injured and dead. The workers were then told to cease work for the day and ordered back to their building (a relief which, as Mr Sadika frankly confesses, was welcome since he was too tired to take much notice of what was happening).

On the following Sunday, two workers were ordered to make a coffin from a few planks, and John was buried. There seems to have been no post-mortem, and there is no evidence that the death was reported. One worker describes a similar death some two months earlier. There appeared to be other graves on the farm.

Mr Sadika does not state whether he was paid the £3 per month for which he contracted. Most of the workers who made statements declare that they never received wages, but one who completed nine months' service says he was paid £14, at the end of that time. Since the others are all escapees, it is possible that those who completed a period of work were paid at the termination.

There seem to have been no visits to the farm during this period by officials who were concerned with the welfare of African workers. If any did pay a visit, the workers were given no opportunity to complain. Mr Sadika became convinced that he would die on the farm, and there is still no information as to the number of Africans who completed their period of service and whether they were released.

When Dorkus Sadika returned with her children from her visit, her husband was not at home. She enquired of friends and neighbours; she asked at the General Hospital; she went to the police, to the Native Commissioner's Court, and to the local gaol. Her husband had disappeared without trace. From October until April, the silence was as profound as that which used to surround the Gestapo's victims.

One of the workers on the farm was Josiah Noko. He had been a taxi driver in Johannesburg, but he had been born in Rhodesia. Arrested one day for failing to produce a valid document, he had been told that unless he could pay his train fare back to Rhodesia he would be sent to work on a farm. He explained that he had money in the bank and in the Post

Office, but he was given no time to withdraw it. And a few days later he met James Sadika. Josiah determined on escape. His first attempt ended in recapture and a beating. But four months after his arrival came a further opportunity. And he escaped. In April 1959 Dorkus Sadika was visited by Josiah, who told her where her husband was.

She told the story to one Joe Goabi, who promptly went to the farm. He asked the farmer whether he could see James Sadika, as he had news for him from home, and after some questions he was taken to the fields. For the first time in six months Mr Sadika received a visitor and was given news of his wife. The conversation had not proceeded far when it was interrupted by the farmer's son, who sent him back to work, and ordered Mr Goabi off the land. Mr Goabi's account of what ensued is that, when he tried to explain to the young man that he had permission from his father to complete the interview, the son drove his jeep against him and forced him physically off the farm, threatening that if he returned he would give him a hiding.

But Mrs Sadika now knew where her husband was. She consulted a lawyer. Affidavits were prepared, and an application was made to the Supreme Court for an order for his release. The farmer was served with a notice to attend the hearing. The attorney who served it upon him asked to see where Sadika had slept, but the request was refused. The farmer filed an affidavit stating that Sadika was free to leave if he wished, but that he desired to complete his six months of service. He asserted that in any event Sadika was obliged to return to the Labour Bureau when he left the farm. (The circular is not specific on this point, but presumably the intention is that, once a contract satisfactory to the Employment Officer has been concluded, the charge is not proceeded with, and no further contract of employment is required.)

On the day of the hearing, Mr Sadika was taken in a car with the farmer, his sons, and a boss boy, and according to his statement he was told that, if he complained in court, he would be killed. When his wife saw him in the foyer of the Court, he was so changed that she hardly recognised him.

He was prevented from speaking to her, and it was not until after he had appeared in the witness box that they had an opportunity of speaking together. The Judge appears to have realised his condition, for he adjourned the hearing so that he might speak with his wife and her counsel, and decide whether he wished to proceed with the application.

Sadika was in a fearful condition. He was thin, dirty and unshaven. He was sobbing and confused, and continually asked to be reassured that he would not be taken back to the farm. At length his wife calmed him. He was taken back into court, and in answer to the Judge, said that he wished to proceed. After a short legal argument, the case was adjourned, and he was released and taken home.

He and other Africans who had undergone this experience were examined by doctors. The findings of the doctors are entirely consistent with their story. Sadika had seven scars on his head (there may have been others), fourteen on his back, and other scars and scabs on other parts of his body. He was severely undernourished, and suffered from a pustular rash on the back and arms, dermatitis and pyorrhoea.

Other Africans have received almost equally horrifying treatment on other farms. Fortunately, the law is more humane than the practice. Where detention on a farm is not in pursuance of a contract freely entered, they are entitled to be released, and the Supreme Court has safeguarded this right. And when it was pointed out publicly, in June 1959, that detentions under the scheme were of questionable legality, many farmers declared that they would have nothing further to do with it.

Mr James Johnston, M.P., asked a question in the British House of Commons, pointing out that Mr Sadika came from Nyasaland and was a British subject. He was told that arrangements existed for the Nyasaland Labour Officer to accompany an official from the Department of Bantu Administration on his inspection, and that the matter was being raised with the South African authorities. Shortly afterwards the South African government appointed a common enquiry into the scheme. The farmer concerned was removed from the list of farmers operating the scheme. No apology or compensation appears to have been offered to the victims.

One fact which seems unlikely to be disputed is that James Sadika was not a political prisoner. His misfortune arose because he belonged to a race which is born to provide cheap labour, and because no one was sufficiently concerned to intervene. What, then, may be expected for those with whom the authorities are indeed concerned?

Portugal

> *The strong men, the masters, regain the pure conscience of a beast of prey; monsters filled with joy, they can return from a fearful succession of murder, arson, rape and torture with the same joy in their hearts, the same contentment in their souls as if they had indulged in some students' rag . . . To judge morality properly, it must be replaced by two concepts borrowed from zoology: the* taming *of a beast and the* breeding *of a specific species.*
>
> Nietzsche: *Zur Genealogie der Moral;* quoted by William Shirer: *The Rise and Fall of the Third Reich*

In Portugal's three universities, Lisbon, Coimbra, and Oporto, the extra-mural activities and associations of the 28,000 students and their teachers are carefully supervised. 'Dismissal, retirement or suspension, and exclusion from examinations or schools are always under the jurisdiction of the Council of Ministers'; 'insubordinate' students are instantly dismissible by the authority of the Ministry of Education. No student may have contact, without Government permission, with any student organisation of another country; domestic student organisations must have their statutes approved by the Ministry of Education, and their officers approved before taking up their duties; and officers of these organisations can be dismissed by the Ministry, if they direct activities against 'academic discipline, the social order, or the higher interests of the country'. They must keep the director of their institution informed of their activities, and authorisation must be obtained for conferences or other events.

In March 1962 the students of Lisbon University applied for permission to hold their annual Student Day celebrations. It was to be an assembly of students from all three universities, and to consist of a football match, a concert, a dinner and a debate. The government failed to answer the application. When some students attempted to assemble notwithstanding, the PIDE, with tear-gas and sub-machine-guns, invested the University premises. Provoked by this interference, 85 per cent of the students of Coimbra and Lisbon came out on strike. Permission to hold the celebrations was then given for the following month, but at the last moment retracted. The strike was resumed and in sympathy the Rector and five of the six heads of faculty resigned. After the strike had lasted for two months, however, the government declared that it was a criminal offence to miss lectures, and arrested 800 students. Successive decree-laws were passed to tighten their administrative authority—which had always been extensive—to the virtually complete degree outlined above.

The students had real complaints, and there was little doctrinal foundation to their resistance. Government grants to students hardly exist, and the majority of those at the Universities necessarily come from richer families. Student associations are expressly non-political; the students asked for the right to hold lectures and social events without prior permission, for the reinstatement of the many professors dismissed for political reasons, for the lifting of the censorship of their own magazines, and for the right to have contracts with international bodies.

But repression of the protesting students necessarily pushes them into a more political position. In the first place, they have to worry about the prospect of earning a living once they graduate, for salaries in the professions are very low indeed in Portugal's perpetually deflated economy. Secondly, where not only are complaints ignored, but the right to make them is denied, and the means of doing so removed, protest logically becomes antagonism to an entire political system.

The following year the government staged a series of trials of the arrested students. One of the first of the student trials, which attracted a great deal of interest although the defendant had in fact ceased to be a member of the University by the time of his arrest, was the trial of Jose Bernadino.

Jose Bernadino, born in Angola of European parents in 1935, entered the Higher Technical Institute of Lisbon University as an engineering student in 1953. From 1957 onwards he held office in a number of student organisations—for which he had government permission—being among other things Vice-President of the Student Association of his faculty, and General Secretary of the Inter-Association of Students, which represents all student bodies. In 1961, fearing arrest, he left the University and went underground.

On 24 May 1962 he was arrested and detained in Aljube prison. He was not allowed to see counsel for six months, and it was a year before he was brought to trial. Attempts were made to extract a confession from him, and there is no reason to doubt the allegations, persisted in by Bernadino himself and by others on his behalf, that he was severely beaten up, and deprived of sleep for two periods of seven and nine continuous days. Charges of police brutality are in their nature almost impossible to corroborate where the government is not interested in having them investigated. But deprivation of sleep for days at a time is a notorious method of the PIDE; it is sometimes referred to as 'the statue'. Such charges, and many far more serious, have been innumerable over the years. And as we saw in an earlier chapter, evidence of their validity has often been impressive enough for distinguished signatories to subscribe to the protests submitted to the Portuguese authorities.

On 9 May 1963 in the Lisbon Special Court, three charges were brought against Bernadino: that he was a member of the Communist Party, that he had directed student subversion as the person responsible for the 'student sector' of Communist Party activities, and that after leaving the University he had engaged in subversive activities while living under a false description. In Portugal the Communist Party is illegal, not because it is specifically proscribed in law but because the government have never given it the necessary permission to exist. Moreover the courts accept the 'notorious fact' that the Communist Party is sworn to the violent overthrow of the State, and that therefore any confessed or convicted Communist is *ex hypothesi* guilty of subversion, whether there is any further evidence of subversive intention or activity against him or not.

In elaboration of the three charges, the prosecution alleged in particular that Bernadino was a ringleader of the student disturbances in Lisbon in the spring of 1962, and that he had taken part in the preparations for a popular uprising, which was alleged, but never established, to have been planned for 28 May 1962.

In the Court there was a prosecuting counsel, who was robed similarly to the judges and who retired with them on each occasion. But he took little part in the proceedings. The questions were put by the President of the Court, and the presentation of the prosecution's case seemed to be a responsibility shared by the President and the principal witness for the prosecution. This witness was a PIDE agent who testified that Bernadino had made an oral confession, before another agent, to the substance of the charges, shortly after his arrest a year earlier. There was no written confession.

The witness further declared that the State possessed certain documents found on Bernadino at the time of his arrest which proved the subversive character of Bernadino's student activities. On the grounds that these documents were secret, and that disclosure would threaten State security, they were not produced in court. Both these pieces of evidence were accepted by the President of the Court. As evidence to establish that Bernadino was concerned with the student unrest of May 1962, the same witness declared that another police officer had seen Bernadino in a car in Lisbon at the time.

When the PIDE had finished this evidence, three witnesses were called to confirm that they had given a lift to Bernadino in the car in question. A woman and her son were unable to identify Bernadino in court, and the husband, who had driven the car, stated positively that Bernadino was definitely not the man to whom he had given a lift. No further evidence was offered by the prosecution.

At the outset of the trial, counsel for the defence submitted to the Court a written statement that admitted Bernadino's membership of the Communist Party, but denied that he was a paid agent of the Party and all charges of engaging in subversive activities. One of the principal witnesses for the defence was to have been a lawyer, Vasco Vieira de Almeida. He was, however, arrested on the morning of the trial, and the defence witnesses consisted of seventeen students who testified that they had known Bernadino well, and that he had never, to the best of their knowledge, engaged in subversive activities during his period at the University.

The witnesses were well-mannered, and in the words of Mr Ronald Waterhouse, Q.C., who attended the trial, 'appeared to be extremely respectable persons'. Their evidence was factual, and quietly delivered. One of the witnesses was in army uniform. However, when any one of them, as several of them did, attempted to testify that the complaints which gave rise to the student disturbances of 1962 were well founded, the witness was roughly interrupted by the Bench on the ground that such testimony was 'Communist propaganda' and a slander on the government, itself an indictable offence.

Bernadino was found guilty of all charges. Before sentence was produced, he was asked if he had anything to say. He was twice interrupted by the President of the Court, and told to confine himself to the facts at issue, and not explain his motives. The third time he began to speak, at a signal from the President of the Court, from eight to ten men in civilian clothes, apparently agents of the PIDE, left their seats at the front of the court, and in the words of Mr Patrick Hallinan, an American attorney who attended the trial, 'set upon Bernadino and beat him to the ground. . . . The beating lasted between three and five minutes, and then Bernadino was carried, apparently unconscious and silent, from the court and did not appear for sentencing.' Mr Waterhouse, Q.C., confirmed this description; he added that the assault 'was of a very violent character, and the force used greatly in excess of that required to remove him'. As Bernadino was carried from Court, an aunt of his called out 'Down with the Fascists'. She was immediately arrested and was subsequently detained in Caxias prison for six months.

In his absence, Bernadino was sentenced to two-and-a-half years in prison, and to 'security measures'. In April 1964 he was further convicted on a charge of using false documents and his sentences were compounded to four years. He has served half his sentence, but without a change in government or government policy he is unlikely ever to be viewed as a politically reliable person, and his prospects of release are very slender. He was in addition deprived of his political rights for fifteen years—a sentence which under the Penal Code forfeits him his right to vote and disqualifies him from any employment in government service, or in any profession requiring a diploma. He was also required to pay 1,000 dollars 'justice costs'.

A curious feature of the trial is that the defence should have admitted membership of the Communist party, when the evidence was no more convincing on this charge than on the others, and the maximum sentence was equally severe. The explanation is probably that, considering conviction and a harsh sentence to be a foregone conclusion whatever the evidence or the plea, the defence preferred to make a defiant statement of political opposition, and include, if allowed, an argument of extenuating circumstance. If they were not allowed to make such an explanation, they would very probably receive some publicity; if they were allowed, they would have succeeded in stating their complaint.

It was a weakness of the defence that they offered no evidence which referred to the time since Bernadino had left the University: but as during that time he had been living underground, this was probably, in the nature of things, impossible to produce. Certainly, the prosecution established no evidence either.

An arrogant act of public brutality (which was, incidentally, illegal since the PIDE have no authority to act inside the courtroom without the Court's explicit instruction) only served to dramatise a process that was judicial only in name.

Nor was this a case of rare severity. On 21 January 1965 thirty students were arrested at dawn in their Lisbon homes. One of these was a fifteen-year-old high-school boy, Jose Augusto Silva, who was kept in a juvenile prison uncharged until, in August, he reached the age of sixteen and became eligible for the attention of the PIDE when he was transferred to the political prison at Caxias. Ana Amorim, a sixteen-year-old schoolgirl, was given a suspended sentence of twelve months and deprived of political rights for five years. A young law student who was arrested, nineteen-year-old Salgado de Matos, was leader of the University Catholic Youth. After weeks of refusal, he was ultimately allowed to receive communion from a Catholic chaplain: he was nevertheless accused of Communism.

One young girl student at the College of Fine Arts, Gina Azevedo, was visited by her father in prison. He had difficulty in recognising her. He wrote to the Ministry of the Interior: 'Her face was that of a corpse; she could not co-ordinate her ideas and had difficulty in the articulation of words. Besides this, she could not stand up properly, but walked clutching the walls. . . .' During her trial she was under psychiatric treatment. Her father's letter was published, and he was summoned to the PIDE and threatened with prosecution for 'damaging the prestige of the country abroad'.

Baeta Neves, a law student, tried to commit suicide by swallowing the lens of his spectacles; Maximio Cunha, a medical student, collapsed and spent thirty-six days in hospital under police supervision. The parents of the students arrested on 21 January wrote a letter to the Minister of Education in which they said: 'We do not wish our children to return home damaged or useless. We have brought our children up to be of value to Portuguese society. We have brought them up to be healthy, we want to receive them home healthy . . . We ask only for humanity. . . .'

A high proportion of arrested students are released after a few months. But they lose a year at the university, and with a record on the police files their chances of any employment are jeopardised, and their chances of employment in any public profession are often negligible. From December 1956 to June 1957, fifty-two young people had been tried in Oporto. Their average age was twenty-two, seven of them were girls, and the youngest under arrest was seventeen. By the time the trial ended, each one, whether found innocent or guilty, had spent over two years in prison since being arrested.

The case of Bernadino is not the worst or the most affecting. It is possible to tell it because there were foreign observers at his trial. Many others—and certainly not only students—have probably been more savagely treated, and with less reason. Many others have been politically more innocent; they have been younger, and their protests less politically formulated. No accounts of their trial are published in Portugal.

The conduct of Bernadino's trial gives an example of a government that attempts to bring, where it has not already brought, all the institutions of a nation to the service of itself. Courts are useful, only if they are corrupt; universities are tolerable, only if they are controlled. It illustrates the helplessness of an individual in a system which has no interest in individuals, or in justice between them, and has the power to pervert the only institutions to which the individual can appeal. And by illustrating these it gives a glimpse into that sordid administrative underworld whose features cannot be listed in the way that statutory laws and constitutional provisions can be listed; which is filled with innumerable untestable charges of insolent, savage, treacherous and unjust behaviour, and equally untestable denials; where power is delegated to agents who have no responsibility; and where that power, with the blessing of government, is left to brutalise and corrupt, as all power does, when there are no institutional restraints upon its exercise.

Conclusion

THESE examples have not been selected with a view to imposing blame. No post-mortem can restore life to the dead, or wasted years to the living. Their purpose is to consider how the first act of legal repression may help to reconcile the public to the loss of freedom, and the first public acceptance of inhumanity will lead to legal provision for tyranny.

But freedom is like economy. Everyone is in favour of the principle, but opposed to particular instances. To believe in freedom is not to believe that one's friends should be free to do as they wish, or those with whom one agrees free to express their views. Believing in freedom is believing in the freedom of one's enemies to walk the earth and to utter words which make one's hackles rise.

'There is no need', wrote George Bernard Shaw, 'to tolerate what appears enlightened or to claim liberty to do what most people consider right. Toleration and liberty have no sense or use except as toleration of opinions that are considered damnable, and liberty to do what seems wrong.'*

Freedom of opinion entails freedom for the opinions of the inarticulate, of cranks, and of devils. The answer to error is not repression.

'Let her and Falsehood grapple; who ever knew Truth put to the wors (*sic*), in a free and open encounter. Her confuting is the best and surest suppressing.' So wrote Milton,† and even if he transpires to be wrong, and falsehood is sometimes the more plausible, the claim of a self-appointed umpire to distinguish them is no solution. Truth is no fragile thing, and is more likely to flourish in robust debate than in a nursery.

Wherever criticism of abuses is possible, and governments may be made uncomfortable, the public conscience is alive. Any protest which will keep it awake is to be welcomed. For during a lull it may fall asleep, and history can point to many communities where its slumber was seen, too late, to be the sleep of death.

* Preface to *The Showing Up of Blanco Posnet*. † *Areopagitica*.

Bibliography

IN ORDER to avoid excessive footnotes, the authors have not indicated specifically their sources for each statement. The following is a brief list of publications to which they are particularly indebted, and it may serve as a basis for further reading.

CHAPTER 2

United Nations Work for Human Rights: United Nations.
A Standard of Achievement: United Nations.
The Rights of the European Citizen: Council of Europe.
The Rule of Law in Modern Society: Norman Marsh; International Commission of Jurists (I.C.J.).
Executive Action and the Rule of Law: I.C.J.
The Dynamic Aspects of the Rule of Law in the Modern Age: I.C.J.
Protection of Human Rights under the Law: Gaius Ezejiofor; Butterworth.
Human Rights Today: Maurice Cranston; Ampersand Ltd.

CHAPTER 3

The United Kingdom

Law of the Constitution: A. V. Dicey; Macmillan.
Law and Opinion in England: A. V. Dicey; Macmillan.
The Queen's Government: Sir Ivor Jennings; Penguin Books.
Freedom, the Individual, and the Law: Harry Street; Penguin Books.

The United States

The Rule of Law in the United States: American Bar Association.
The Living U.S. Constitution: Saul K. Padover; Mentor Books, Praeger.
Civil Liberties and the Constitution: Paul G. Kamper; University of Michigan Press.
Justice in the American South: Anthony Lester; Amnesty International.

The Soviet Union

The Communist Manifesto: The Communist Party.

Lenin and Stalin on the State: Lawrence & Wishart, Ltd.

Government, Law and Courts in the Soviet Union and Eastern Europe: Gsovski and Grzybowski; Atlantic Books, Stevens.

The Communist Theory of Law: H. Kelson; Stevens.

Soviet Legal Theory: R. Schlesinger; Kegan Paul.

The Soviet System of Government: John N. Hazard; University of Chicago Press.

The Origins of the Communist Autocracy: Leonard Schapiro; Praeger.

Ghana

Politics in Ghana 1946–1960: Austin; Oxford University Press.

Constitutional Law of Ghana: Bennion; Butterworth.

Socialism in Ghana: A Political Interpretation: Essay by Colin Legum in *African Socialism*; Friedland and Rosberg: Oxford University Press.

Kwame Nkrumah of Ghana: Essay by Ronald Segal in *African Profiles*; Penguin Books.

Ghana: Essay by Anthony Sampson in *Common Sense about Africa*; Gollancz.

Africa Today and Tomorrow: John Hatch; Dobson.

Democracy and the New African States: Essay by Carl Rosberg, Jr., in *African Affairs*; St Antony's Papers No. 15; Chatto & Windus.

Consciencism: Kwame Nkrumah; Heinemann.

Bulletin of I.C.J., No. 8 (Dec. 1958), No. 13 (May 1962), No. 18 (March 1964).

The Republic of South Africa

South Africa and the Rule of Law: I.C.J.

Prison Conditions: Amnesty International.

The Rise of the South African Reich: Brian Bunting; Penguin Books.

The Tragedy of Apartheid: Norman Phillips; Allen & Unwin.

Portugal

Doctrine and Action: Dr. Salazar; Faber & Faber.

Structure and Growth of the Portuguese Economy: V. Xavier Pintado; EFTA.

Oldest Alley—Portrait of Salazar's Portugal: Fryer and McGowan Pinheiro; Dobson.

Portugal and its Empire—the Truth: Antonio de Figueredo; Gollancz.

Portugal's Political Prisoners: Lord Gardiner; *Daily Telegraph*, 10 February 1964.

Bulletin of I.C.J., No. 8 (Dec. 1958), No. 13 (May 1962).

Chapter 4

The United Kingdom

Gangrene: Peter Benenson and others; Calder.

The United States

Grand Inquest: Telford Taylor; Ballantine Books.

The Un-Americans: Frank J. Donner; Ballantine Books.

The Fifth Amendment Today: Erwin N. Griswold; Harvard University Press.

The Soviet Union

The Bluebottle: Valeriy Tarsis; Collins and Harvill: Dutton.

Ward 7: Valeriy Tarsis; Collins and Harvill.

The Republic of South Africa

South Africa and the Rule of Law; I.C.J.